Rethymnon

A British couple's true story of love and loss on Crete

Rethymnon

A British couple's true story of love and loss on Crete

Marilyn Drawwater

Rethymnon

Published by The Conrad Press Ltd. in the United Kingdom 2022

Tel: +44(0)1227 472 874
www.theconradpress.com
info@theconradpress.com

ISBN 978-1-914913-47-1

Typesetting and Cover Design by: Charlotte Mouncey, www.bookstyle.co.uk
Cover created with author's own photographs and from istockphoto.com
The Conrad Press logo was designed by Maria Priestley.

Printed and bound in Great Britain by Clays Ltd, Elcograf S.p.A.

For Robin, my love and my inspiration
19 December 1945 - 7 April 2018
I miss you every minute of every day

Contents

Preface

My first history lesson at grammar school was based on the Minoans of Crete. Little did I know then that I would one day wind up living here!

When I first met Robin I was twenty-one, he was twenty-nine and already had a family. I know my father had grave doubts about me taking on a readymade family, especially at such a young age, but he came to accept Robin when he could see what a good husband Robin was and how happy he made me. Even though we had both had bad experiences in our past, we simply knew we were right for each other and never had any doubts. We lived together for two years before getting married, which was quite daring back in 1975! Just being together was what was important. In all, we had forty-three happy years together.

Robin could be quite outspoken and I must admit I sometimes worried that he might cause offence. He said at least people knew where they stood with him, what they saw was what they got and people did seem to respect him for that. It was his belief that one of the reasons our marriage was so successful was because we never tried to change each other. Each accepted the other person as they were faults and all. Although there was a considerable age difference between us, we never really noticed it. Of course, we had our arguments as all couples do but they never affected the deep, abiding love we felt for each other.

We first visited Greece in 1998 when we stayed on Rhodes. We liked it so much we spent the next few years exploring various Greek islands. Even after we started to visit more exotic locations, such as the Caribbean and South East Asia, we came back to Greece for a week every June to celebrate our wedding anniversary.

As we reached an age when it was necessary to consider our future in relation to retirement, we began to worry about how we would fund that retirement. This was part of what drove our plan to retire to a Greek island. We discovered that the cost of living was much lower. That, coupled with the better climate, made the prospect very attractive. Of course, at that time retirement still seemed a long way in the future.

Full retirement was never in our minds. We started to dream about Robin sitting on the seafront painting pictures to sell to tourists, while I would write a book. Robin often used to say he was just a simple carpenter but he was much more than that. He was a master craftsman. If it was possible to make something out of wood, he could do it. Robin not doing some form of woodwork was something I could never imagine, even if it was just for his own satisfaction rather than for pay.

I have always been an avid reader and also kept a diary of some sort for most of my life. It has always been my ambition to write a book but, every time I started to put pen to paper or fingers to the keyboard, life has got in the way. My career in the law gave me some opportunity to hone my literary skills, when drafting documents or preparing for a court hearing. When my work contract came to an end in March 2020, I saw this as an ideal opportunity to start on what was intended to be a novel. I embarked on a creative writing course. This led me in a slightly different direction. My study started with writing articles and short stories for magazines. I soon discovered that selling articles and stories to magazines was much more difficult than I anticipated. The course even included a short foray into journalism but I decided this was not for me. It was the assignment on planning a non-fiction book that gave me the idea of telling my story and Robin's. Now I have fulfilled my ambition to write a book and have not given up on the idea of writing a novel.

We finally decided to make the move when we visited in 2017 to celebrate our Ruby Wedding Anniversary. During that week we looked at various properties but were reluctant to put down a deposit until we had funding in place. On our return to the UK, we booked another two week holiday to Crete in September; with the intention of setting everything up to move later in the year. Miraculously we were able to do this. The main difficulty was finding accommodation. By this time we had decided to rent. Rethymnon is a university town and most of the apartments are let to Airbnb in summer and students in the winter.

Now the race was really on! We left Crete in early October and planned to return to live here permanently in mid-November, so we had a lot to do in a few short weeks. We managed it – just! There were a number of difficulties we encountered and the book explains how we overcame these.

Living in a tourist area in winter is very different to visiting for a couple of weeks in the summer. Robin, in particular, loved it. We were lucky to get a mild winter and the book talks about how we settled in and enjoyed things such as Christmas and Rethymnon Carnival.

Sadly, on our first visit back to the UK to see our family, Robin was taken ill and died suddenly. This book is my tribute to him and my way of keeping his memory alive. This is both a happy story and a sad one and I hope you will enjoy reading all of it.

Marilyn Drawwater – February 2022

Chapter 1 – Greek island holidays

'All Greek islands are the same,' a colleague of Robin's once said to him, 'they are barren and nothing but rocks.'

This is simply not true. They each have their own character.

We were never able to afford foreign holidays when our children were young, so our experience of travelling abroad came later in life than most couples. I was in my thirties and Robin in his forties when we had our first holiday abroad, on Malta. There followed a number of years on Malta with my parents. The four of us got along very well although Robin was frequently subjected to some leg pulling from my father. He took it all in good part.

We had some good times and some laughs. I can remember my father 'moon walking' across the living area of our apartment. On another occasion we went to our favourite restaurant in Sleima. Robin ordered whitebait for a starter and was clearly not paying attention when the waiter, with a completely straight face, asked if he wanted it filleted and Robin said, 'Yes.' My father never let him forget that! My mother was only four foot ten inches tall. We went for a meal one evening and she ordered prawn cocktail. The glass was so tall she had to stand up to eat her starter!

As my parents began to age, they realised holidaying together was no longer a viable prospect. They wanted to sleep in the afternoons; Robin and I wanted to sight-see. That was when we struck out on our own and had our first taste of Greece.

We started with Rhodes, mainly because of its connection with the Knights of St John and Malta. Most people think of Malta when they think of the Order of St John but the Knights Hospitaller were on Rhodes long before they went to Malta.

Our first sight of the Old Town of Rhodes took our breath away. The hotel we stayed at was in the new town so it was just a short walk into the Old Town. We turned the corner and there it was spread out before us. After the first couple of days settling in, we walked into the Old Town every evening for a meal. We found the narrow cobbled streets and old buildings magical and very romantic. Mandraki harbour is lovely. There is a spit of land containing three windmills and I have always had an interest in windmills. As a child I often said I would live in a windmill when I grew up. Two statues of deer guard the entrance which, at one time, would have been straddled by the Colossus.

I had a slightly worrying experience on our way back to the hotel one night as we were walking along the harbour. Robin decided he needed to make use of the public conveniences so I waited on the seafront. He seemed to be gone for a very long time and I started walking up and down. This obviously gave entirely the wrong impression because a car started to slow down by the kerbside just as Robin returned. I had never been so pleased to see him in my life. Jokingly, I told him if he had been a bit longer I could have earned some extra spending money!

Staying on Rhodes was also our first experience of hiring a car in a country where driving is on the right. The first time we stayed there we hired one just for a day at a time because Rhodes is quite a small island and we liked spending time in the Old Town. The first car we hired was somewhat the worse for wear. Every time we went over a bump in the road, the sun-roof flew open! While exploring the countryside, we met a coach coming towards us. Robin said, 'Look at that idiot; he's on the wrong side of the road!'

I replied, 'No, Robin – you are!'

He had forgotten to keep to the right!

Luckily he was able to pull over in time. We liked Rhodes so much we returned two years later for another holiday. It felt like coming home. On our first evening we went out for a meal in the Old Town, clinked our glasses together and said, *'Yammas!'* It was like being on honeymoon. I took on a readymade family when I met Robin and we could not afford a honeymoon. He always said it did not matter because our life together was like one long honeymoon.

Our next Greek island holiday was Kefalonia. It is on the other side of the Greek mainland and has a completely different character. We hired a car for the whole two weeks this time and Robin did not have any further mishaps – at least not with the car...

Opposite our hotel was a restaurant called the Olive Grove. As well as serving meals, the bar was open to the public so, even if we were not eating there, we would pop in for a cocktail before going on to our chosen restaurant. The bar tender got to know us well. When we sat at the bar she would say, 'Do you trust me?' to which we would both reply, 'No!'

In spite of this, she would always prepare us a special cocktail which usually meant her leaving a bottle of spirits upended in the glass while she prepared the other ingredients! She gave us both a large hug goodbye on our last night.

While staying on Kefalonia we had a day trip on the car ferry to Ithaca which was an interesting experience. First of all, we were told to visit the monastery. So we drove up and up a narrow winding road along the mountainside with a sheer drop on one side. Suddenly, we ran out of road and all that was left was a gravel track. Fortunately, Robin was an excellent driver and it did not faze him one bit. It was just as well he did not have his eyes tight shut like I did! When we arrived, the view was well worth the drive up.

At the time we bought our ferry tickets at Kefalonia we could not buy a return. We were told to purchase our return tickets on Ithaca. What we did not realise was that this had to be done when we docked. By the time we were ready to return and tried to buy tickets for the return trip, the ticket office was closed. Our only option was to get on the ferry and hope we could pay then. Robin managed to park the car behind a couple of lorries so we could not be made to get off.

When a crew member asked for our tickets and found we did not have any, Robin was hauled off before the captain. I thought he would be thrown in the brig! As it turned out, he was not the only one. They all got a dressing down by the captain, who was apparently a large man with a beard and somewhat intimidating, but this was clearly a regular occurrence and Robin was able to pay the captain for our return tickets.

The next time we visited a Greek island we stayed on Kos. This was the last time we caught the tour operator's bus from the airport. We arrived in the evening and were directed to our coach where we sat for over an hour waiting for another flight to land. The tour operator then took us all over the island dropping people off at various hotels. We were the last drop off at 6 a.m. the next day. We later found out that our hotel was actually the closest to the airport. After that, we always took a taxi from the airport or had a hire car waiting for us.

Kos was not our favourite Greek island but we did enjoy sitting in restaurants along the seafront in the evening. Wherever we went we would look at the moon and the North Star and realise our friends and family, over 1,000 miles away, would be looking at the same things. I still believe that when I look up at the moon and stars in the place he loved that Robin is looking down at me.

One day there was an important England football match. Neither Robin nor I were interested in football, so we walked from one end of the town to the other trying to find a restaurant not showing football on television. We eventually found a Chinese restaurant without a television. No sooner had we sat down than there was a power cut that lasted most of the evening: so that put paid to the football! Although it did not bother us, we did feel sorry for all the England fans on holiday there who had been disappointed.

We were also fascinated by watching the fire-fighting helicopter drawing water from the sea to extinguish a forest fire. It was only when we drove through the countryside later in the week that we saw the devastation caused by the fire. It certainly brought home to us how careful one needs to be when the weather is so hot and dry. It made us thankful that we had stopped smoking several years previously.

The following year we went to Zante (also known as Zakynthos). One thing I have noticed is that the Greeks often have more than one name for the same place; which can be a bit confusing. We stayed in the main resort but, luckily for us, our hotel was outside the tourist area so it was reasonably quiet. It was our stay on Zante that led to our decision to move to a Greek island, but that is for another chapter.

The highlight of our stay here was seeing the turtles. When we booked our tickets, we were warned that there was no guarantee we would see any. Of course, neither of us realised that we would have to wade out to the boat. Instead of being sensible and wearing our swimsuits, Robin was in a T-shirt and shorts and I was in a cotton suit with a short skirt. By the time we got to the boat, Robin's shorts and my skirt were soaked. It did not matter, though, because the water was beautifully clear and warm and it was a pleasure to walk in it. We soon dried out in the hot sun. It was certainly worth it because we saw several giant turtles that came very close to the boat.

That brings us to Crete. We had wanted to visit the largest of the Greek islands for some time but were unable to get a weekend flight. Because he was self-employed, Robin did not want to take the extra days off work that travelling mid-week would mean and I did not want to use up any more days of my precious annual leave. We leapt at the chance when weekend flights became available.

The first time we stayed on Crete, we were self-catering at Stalis (or Stalida). This was the next village to Malia, the haunt of Club 18-30, so was very tourist-orientated. Nevertheless, there were some extremely nice restaurants and a lovely cocktail garden we visited each evening before our meal. Of course we visited Knossos, Phaestos and the palace at Malia. In addition, there were lots of other places to see. Agios Nikolaos is a very nice town with a lagoon and a pretty little bridge over it. The Lassithi Plateau with its windmills is not to be missed. Irapetra in the south, with its ruined fort, is also worth a visit. Stalis also has one of the best beaches on the island.

It was in Stalis that we had our first taste of raki. We were sitting outside a restaurant overlooking the sea. An elderly Cretan man was sitting at a table by the beach most of the evening, pouring drinks from something that appeared to be a lemonade bottle. He got up to leave and, as he passed our table, he poured us each a glass, said *Yammas* and walked out. It was certainly not lemonade! Over the years we acquired quite a taste for raki.

There was a gift shop near where we were staying. Every time we passed, a toy outside was programmed to say, 'Ha, ha, ha, ha, I love you.' After our return home Robin got in the habit of calling me during my lunch-break and saying, 'Ha, ha, ha, ha, I love you.'

While staying at Stalis we were advised to visit the Rethymnon area but it was too far away for a day trip. The following year we decided to return to Crete but stay in Rethymnon. We fell in love with the town. On our arrival in the early hours, after collecting our hire car at the airport, we had some difficulty in finding our hotel. We stopped near the Municipal Gardens to ask for directions and discovered it was almost right in front of us! The hotel kitchen was closed so we bought cheese pies and fresh orange juices from one of the kiosks that appear to be open twenty four hours a day. We then sat on the wall opposite the hotel to eat and drink them.

Rethymnon is the third largest town on Crete but its Old Town is the largest. We were enchanted with it from the start. On our first evening we went to the Venetian harbour. In the summer it is surrounded by fish restaurants. We had a very enjoyable meal there but, due to their location, the restaurants are quite expensive compared to those in the town. However, it was a lovely way to spend our first evening. After that, we tended to have a cocktail at the hotel bar or on the seafront and then go into the Old Town for a meal.

It is not uncommon to be treated to an impromptu concert, when some of the locals get together and start playing the Cretan lyra, guitars and singing. The atmosphere is hard to describe – it has to be experienced.

We loved Rethymnon so much that a few years later we started spending a week here every June to celebrate our wedding anniversary. I can remember sitting at a bar on the Beach Road in the evening and gazing out across the sea towards the harbour, watching the lively atmosphere and the palm trees. These are not native to Crete but have been imported due to their hardy nature. I said to Robin, 'We just have to live here.'

Chapter 2 – Why we decided to emigrate and why we chose Crete

Robin was a first-class carpenter and joiner. His last job working for an employer was with a shop-fitting company. Although he enjoyed the work, he did not like travelling all over the country and only being home at weekends. He missed being with his family. After much discussion between us, he finally decided to start working for himself. It was a risk, of course, but worked out well. His skill spoke for itself and he found plenty of work either subcontracting or taking on his own jobs. He never had to advertise.

One of the downsides of being self-employed was that he had no pension provision. He took out a personal pension plan which, at the time, should have provided approximately two-thirds of his income on retirement. Over the next twenty years or so this was eroded into next to nothing because it was not index-linked. The same thing happened to me. Although I had a reasonable occupational pension, even with our state pensions we could not look forward to a reasonable standard of living on retirement.

We considered downsizing and moving to the coast or the country. The prospect of living in a coastal town where the majority of the residents were retirees did not appeal; nor did moving to the country. Robin came from a small town in Lincolnshire and hated living in the country. I had always lived in a big town. I was born in Southend-on-Sea in Essex and moved to South West London with my parents when I was sixteen. My parents retired to the country. When my father died, my mother had no choice. She had to move to sheltered housing because she could not drive and there was no public transport where she had lived with my father.

The solution to our retirement dilemma came when we were holidaying on Zante. As I mentioned in Chapter 1, we stayed just outside the tourist area and often walked into town during the day. We would stop off at a bar near the hotel for a drink and snack at lunchtime. The barman was English and we often got chatting to him. He told us he had been made redundant while in his sixties; he could not get another job because of his age but still had a mortgage, so he decided to sell up and move to Zante. The cost of living is much lower on the Greek islands; he was able to work part time in the bar, do a bit of gardening and walk people's dogs. Putting that all together, it provided him with sufficient income to live comfortably and even eat out a couple of times a week.

This gave us food for thought. We discussed it between ourselves during the rest of the holiday but it was put on the back-burner for a while when we returned to our busy lives. After all, we had plenty of time before we were ready to retire...

When we first moved there, Surbiton was a very nice place to live. There is a fast train service to Waterloo, so we could be in central London in twenty minutes. On the other hand, we could jump in the car and be in the country in about the same length of time. We would often walk along the Thames from Surbiton to Kingston, watching the river traffic and the swans and geese, then have lunch at a riverside pub. Alternatively, we could get on the small ferry across the Thames and walk in the opposite direction to Hampton Court.

We loved Hampton Court for different reasons. Robin was interested in the architecture and I was fascinated by the history. Cooking was one of Robin's hobbies and he was a talented amateur chef. He loved it when the Tudor kitchens were open to the public so he could see how people cooked in those times. Richmond Park was also close by and we spent many an afternoon walking through the park and watching the deer. Robin often played golf on one of the two courses there.

Things deteriorated over the years. When we first moved to Surbiton, most families only had one car. Gradually, it became normal for husband and wife to have a car each, then grown-up children started to have their own vehicles. I have to admit that, in addition to the family car, Robin had a van for work and at one stage his son also had a car parked on the driveway. With public transport becoming increasingly unreliable, having one's own transport became a necessity. I cannot ride a bike so that was never an option for me. However, this all meant that the roads became busier and busier, leading to constant traffic snarl-ups.

As well as this, many buildings that made up the town's history were torn down and characterless blocks of flats put in their place. It broke our hearts when the Red Lion pub, that gave Red Lion Road its name, was demolished and replaced by what must be one of the ugliest buildings in London. What used to be a lovely suburban town had completely lost its character.

When we moved into our house in 1984 I remember saying, 'That's it, I never want to move again, you will be carrying me out of here in a box!'

Although we loved our house, the changes in the town over the next thirty years made us realise that it was no longer where we wanted to end our days.

In September 2008 we toured Vietnam. After looking at the itinerary, we realised this was to be an experience rather than a holiday! To get some relaxation in beforehand, we spent a week on Rhodes in June to celebrate our wedding anniversary. We gave some serious consideration to settling on Rhodes. It was the first Greek island we had visited and we were fascinated with the Old Town. Robin was a Chevalier and I was (and still am) a Dame of the Order of St John so we had an interest in the connection, especially the Street of the Knights. We never tired of wandering through the Old Town and ate there every evening.

Then in June 2010 we spent a week in Rethymnon and realised that Crete was a much better option. Although we liked Rhodes very much, we felt that it was too small and we would soon feel claustrophobic. We also had to take into account what we would do in winter. Crete is a much bigger island and Rethymnon, being a university town, does not close down completely in the winter. From this time on, a week in Rethymnon in June became a regular feature.

We usually took our summer holidays in September but in 2013, due to our commitments with the Order of St John, we could not get away until late October. This was a good opportunity to see Crete outside the usual holiday season. The weather was still good but some things were beginning to close down for the winter. A lot of the sun-beds from the beach had already been stored away at the end of the season. For the first four days, we stayed in a hotel in Elounda on the opposite side of the island to Rethymnon. We thought we should try another part of Crete to make sure Rethymnon was really where we wanted to settle.

We enjoyed those four days very much, even though the website misrepresented how close the hotel was to the town. If we did not want to drive, so we could have a glass of wine with our meal in the evening, we had to take a taxi into town. During our later years on Malta, we did have half board in the hotel because this was easier for my parents as they got older, but we were never interested in all-inclusive. I can see how this may appeal to families with young children but we always wanted to try the local food and soak up the atmosphere. We especially enjoyed eating at a seafood restaurant set on a raft in the harbour.

Nevertheless, it was a nice hotel, the staff were very friendly and the view was magnificent. The barman even insisted on having his photo taken with us. There were also a lot of places of interest to visit nearby. Over the few days we were there, it became apparent that this was a village where there would be very little happening in the winter. Agios Nikolaos, nearby, is a larger town but we still felt the pull towards Rethymnon.

In the middle of the first week, we travelled on to Rethymnon. We had planned to stop for lunch on the way but found it took us much less time than anticipated, driving along the National Road. On arrival, it immediately felt like coming home. Before checking into our hotel, we walked along by the harbour and had grilled prawns with a glass of white wine in one of the seafood restaurants. Looking across the harbour and watching the fish in the clear blue water, taking in the smell of garlic, thyme and grilled fish, there was no doubt; Rethymnon was where we wanted to live.

Chapter 3 – The decision

Although we had decided to move to Crete when we retired, we had to wait until we were both in receipt of our state pensions. We would need these to live on, at least until we had another source of income. Robin was older than me and became eligible in 2010. He considered deferring his pension but the advantages of doing so were so negligible, he decided to take his pension on reaching retirement age, which enabled him to work shorter hours. He was able to do more specialised joinery work, which was what he enjoyed. Our initial idea was to rent out our house in Surbiton and rent a property in Rethymnon.

We celebrated our Ruby Wedding Anniversary on 4 June 2017. As usual we came to Crete for a week. We arrived on Saturday 3 June. After travelling most of the day before, we decided to take it easy on Sunday, which was our wedding anniversary. We had a walk in the Old Town, a spot of lunch, and then returned to the hotel for a swim and a rest. In the evening we had champagne in the hotel bar before heading out to eat. Because it was a very special occasion, we went to one of the seafood restaurants at the harbour.

When the waiter found out it was our wedding anniversary, he took us up to a balcony overlooking the harbour. There was only one table on the balcony and we had a wonderful seafood platter with a nice bottle of wine. When dining out Robin would often say (in the remains of his Lincolnshire accent), 'I have a nice bottle of wine, good food and a *bootiful* woman. What more do I want?'

Looking down over the beautiful Venetian harbour and taking in the atmosphere was really romantic. It was an evening to remember, for which I am really grateful because it turned out to be our last anniversary together.

This was the year when I became eligible for the state pension and Robin, in particular, was fired up to start sorting out how we were going to achieve the move. While shopping for anniversary presents for each other, he started looking in estate agents. We saw a house in the Old Town advertised at such a low price we could have bought it out of our savings. On enquiring, however, we were advised not to buy a property in the Old Town because the preservation regulations were very strict and would cause us all sorts of problems. Robin could understand that, having worked on listed buildings in the UK.

During the course of that week we looked at a number of properties. The problem we found was that all the properties in the town were apartments. If we wanted a villa, we would have to live in a village. This did not really appeal to us. We did look at one apartment in the town but were put off by the broken glass in the entrance hall window and the fact that the lift was out of order. Walking up the stairs was not a problem for us but it spoke of a general lack of maintenance.

A couple of days later we went to one of our favourite restaurants for a meal. Sadly, it is no longer in business. It was in the heart of the Old Town and called the Melody Garden. There was a downstairs restaurant but, unless the weather was really bad, we would eat upstairs in the garden under the grape vine and the stars. I recall on that night Robin came out with one of his silly remarks that I am sure he made just to see me laugh. We were talking about international cuisine and he said, 'I don't like that German sausage, that weasel wurt.'

I nearly fell off my chair laughing and could not stop. How had he managed to convert *Bratwurst* to weasel wurt? Of course, I have since realised he was thinking about the wiener wurst popular in America! He just looked at me and said, 'I love to see you laugh.'

If the restaurant was not too busy, the manager would often bring the raki bottle over to our table and we would sit there until the early hours putting the world to rights. On this occasion, when we said we were looking for property, he said he had a friend who was in real estate. We agreed that he could give his friend my mobile phone number. Robin tended to leave his mobile switched off in the hotel safe so he was not bothered by business calls when he was on holiday.

We were contacted the next day and an appointment made at the real estate office. Pictures of various properties were shown to us and we were amazed to see that we could buy a villa with two bedrooms, two bathrooms and a swimming pool for less than half the value of our house in Surbiton. The only downside was that they were all in villages and not the town. We went to look at two of them. One, in particular, appealed to us because it had a workshop that Robin could use for his woodwork. At least it was on a bus route so we could get into town by public transport if we did not want to drive.

Although by this time we were both of state retirement age, neither of us was ready to retire completely. We had the idea that we could take out an equity release on our house in Surbiton, buy a villa on Crete and rent it out to holidaymakers until we were ready to move. Once we were ready to make the move we would rent out our house in Surbiton.

We were introduced to a Greek lawyer who started to put the wheels in motion but, fortunately for us, we did not put down a deposit. After contacting one of the financial institutions offering equity release, we were told they would be quite happy to lend us the money to buy a holiday home, but we were required to continue living in the house in Surbiton and not rent it out. This put paid to our house purchase in Crete, a fact I was to be grateful for later.

On our return home we did briefly consider selling our house to fund the purchase of the villa. However, I felt pressured by the real estate agent and did not want to rush into anything. I contacted the Greek lawyer and explained to her that we had not been able to raise the funding and not to take any further action unless she heard from us. She seemed to think this was sensible and I got the impression she also thought we had been pressurised.

This did not mean that we had given up on our dream. We booked another two weeks on Crete at the end of September/ beginning of October. In those two weeks we hoped to be able to sort out our residents' permits and find somewhere to live.

Shortly after our return home, we attended an investiture into the Order of St John. It took place on a Saturday at a church near the British Museum. Robin and I decided to make a weekend of it and stay at a hotel from the Friday to the Sunday. We took a day off on the Friday and arrived early so we could have a look round; find the church and the hotel where the dinner was take place afterwards. Quite by chance, we found a Greek restaurant where we decided to have our evening meal on the Friday. It was a lovely evening. Robin was telling all the staff that we were going to move to Crete and they even had raki! This made us even more determined to make the move.

I started looking at the requirements online and also for rental properties. The UK Government website was helpful. It explained that we needed a Greek bank account, proof of income and health insurance. Greece has a reciprocal arrangement for healthcare with the NHS for people in receipt of UK pensions. The problem was that the government would only send out the necessary forms once we were living on Crete. They did advise that in the interim we could use our European Health Insurance Cards. Doctors were people we avoided if at all possible so we had never had these before but I applied for them straight away.

I soon discovered that no-one in Greece does anything online. Even where people have email addresses, they never answer emails. Everything is done either in person or by phone. Having a total of about five words of Greek, I did not feel confident about speaking to Greek people by phone even if they did speak good English.

The only sites where I could find properties for rent were holiday lets. Our only option was to hope we could get everything done during our two-week stay at the end of September. I contacted the Greek lawyer and she agreed to help us apply for our residents' permits and anything else we needed. She was very good and charged us very little. Another thing we soon noticed was that Greek people tend to say their English is not very good and then go on to speak it fluently!

Our idea was to find temporary accommodation so that we could put our house on the market and have plenty of time to look around on Crete to find something to buy. Our mortgage was paid off and the proceeds of sale would allow us to buy two reasonable-sized properties on Crete and one small one. We could then live in one and rent out the other two, thus giving us another source of income.

Robin even thought about buying an old property that needed work so that he could project manage the renovation.

He would enjoy that and it would give him something to do, although quite how he would have managed it without being able to speak any Greek I am not sure! Even at that stage, I had reservations about selling our house. We contacted agents to value it for both sale and rental purposes.

Although we had often spoken about retiring to Crete, at this stage, we did not tell our family or my employer what we had planned in case it fell through.

Chapter 4 – We did everything in two weeks

At the end of September 2017 we set off on our now familiar journey. We drove to Gatwick early on the Saturday morning. In earlier years, we had been reluctant to leave our car in an airport car park but we realised that it was much simpler, and cheaper, than having a taxi both ways. People are very quick to recount horror stories of cars being used by staff for their own private use and the owners coming back to find the mileage had significantly increased. If this happens at all, I suspect it is rarely. We found the system to be a good one and the car secure.

After getting through bag drop and security, we settled down to a light breakfast while waiting for our departure gate to be announced. Even though this was going to be a working holiday, we still had a sense of excitement about visiting Crete again. Robin found flying boring once we were at 35,000 feet and there was not much to see, so he usually went to sleep. I always found it difficult to sleep on the plane; I could never find a comfortable position, so I always had several books on my Kindle. We were both always pleased to be told we were about to start our descent into Heraklion.

As soon as the plane touched down at Heraklion's Kazantzakis Airport, we were home. The bright sunshine hit us as soon as we emerged from the plane and we were impatient to be on our way, fretting at the delays going through the passport check, baggage reclaim and picking up our hire car.

By this time we knew the way to Rethymnon. It is a lovely drive along the coast from Heraklion, with the mountains on one side and the deep blue of the sea on the other. We were at our hotel in no time. The staff all knew us and welcomed us back. Robin was anxious to get into our room and unpacked so he could change into his shorts! I could never get him to wear shorts in the UK, even on rare hot days, but it was always the first thing he wanted on holiday.

We had parked the car and would not be using it for a couple of days because we could not start 'work' until Monday, so next stop was the hotel bar and Robin's first pint of the Greek beer he liked. The barman remembered us well. He shook Robin's hand and gave me a hug. There was a particular table out by the pool area that we liked to sit at if it was free. We sat there with our drinks, looking out over the blue Cretan sea, watching the holidaymakers walk past and thought things could not get better than this.

The waiting staff all welcomed us like old friends when we went down to breakfast the next morning. This was in spite of the fact that we only had bed and breakfast and had never stayed in the hotel for lunch or an evening meal. There were large umbrellas to shade the sun so we preferred to eat our breakfast outside. On one occasion, we had a table very close to the pool and I wondered if this was the occasion when Robin was going to get his shirt wet (I will explain this later in the chapter)! After spending a large part of his working life walking about on roof beams; unlike me, he had very good balance so managed to avoid falling in the pool.

There was always a good breakfast buffet. On Sundays, guests were greeted with a glass of champagne, so this was a great start to our working holiday. We would then be seated and served with orange juice and our choice of tea or coffee. Everyone's taste was catered for. Fried food, such as bacon and sausages, was available. Eggs and omelettes were cooked fresh to order at the serving-hatch. There were also cereals, fresh fruit, yoghurt, cheese and cold meats, bread, conserves and a Cretan corner serving local specialities. The only problem was trying to avoid eating too much! Robin always liked his fry-up with eggs and bacon although he was not so keen on the spicy sausages.

I contacted our Greek lawyer on the Monday and we made an appointment for Tuesday. She was very helpful and made several telephone calls to find out for certain what documents we needed to apply for residents' permits. Something I have since learned is that, in Greece, even when you think you have everything you could possibly need; there is always something else the officials ask for. When we left the lawyer's office I remember saying to Robin, 'We are really going to do this!'

Our first task was to open a Greek bank account. For a couple of years, we had gone to a seafood restaurant on the

Beach Road for our wedding anniversary. The head waiter was always helpful and recommended a good wine to accompany the fish. After he left, we stopped going there but were pleased to find he had now opened his own restaurant. Naturally, we went there for a meal and, when we explained that we were now ready to move to Crete, he offered to take us to his bank.

He introduced us but had to leave as he had work to do for his restaurant. He also said that, if we needed a Greek address, we could use the address of his restaurant. Greek banks are nothing like English ones. Everyone is shouting across the office and eating at their desks. It took us a while to find the right person and then discovered we needed a tax number, although we could use our UK address to open the account.

The next stop then was back to the lawyer and we made an appointment to meet her at the tax office. Robin was a bit obsessive about not being late anywhere. This usually resulted in us arriving everywhere about half an hour early. He found it difficult to come to terms with everyone on Crete turning up late, even professionals such as lawyers and accountants. We sat in the foyer of the tax office wondering if we were in the right place when I received an email from our lawyer to say she was running late.

Thank goodness she was there to sort things out for us. She pushed her way to the front of the queue to get the forms we needed to complete and then translated them into English for us. It was here that we needed the address of our friend's restaurant because we had to have a Greek address to get a tax number. To our surprise, we were issued with our numbers straight away.

I think the worst part of the two weeks was dealing with

the bank. Because Greece has not yet entered the digital age, most people have to go to the bank or post office to pay their bills. There is a queuing system for this but, for anything else; it seems to be a free for all. People just push their way in, even when it is not their turn, and not being able to speak Greek was a disadvantage.

We managed to get seen eventually and opened a joint bank account. I had encountered some difficulty trying to access our bank account online from the hotel, so the bank clerk allowed me to use the bank's computer to transfer the necessary funds into our new account. She told us that we were moving to Crete from the UK and at the same time, she was planning to move to the UK to live with her English boyfriend!

Most of the next couple of weeks was spent trying to find accommodation but this will be dealt with in more detail in the next chapter. We did find some time for relaxation in between. On one occasion we visited Lake Kournas. This is a popular spot for tourists and locals alike. It is a wildlife sanctuary. Pedaloes and canoes can be hired but they are not to be beached near the nesting grounds for the various wildlife.

Robin refused to hire a pedalo this time because I nearly pushed him in by accident the last time we went out on the lake. That was not the first time. Being nervous of water, I had grabbed him and nearly pushed him in when we went into a cave in Kefalonia in a small boat. That was when he said I am not safe by boats and one day he would end up getting his shirt wet!

We shared a Greek salad. I had a glass of wine but Robin stuck to Fanta lemon because he was driving. On Sundays local families visit the lake in large groups and eat spit roasted lamb with fried potatoes. Crete is very family orientated and family members of all age groups enjoy getting together on a regular basis. Cretan children tend to eat the same as the adults and do not expect their own menu, although a number of tourist establishments have a children's menu for visitors.

During my online searches before returning in September, I did manage to contact the Cretan International Community (CIC). This is a society for ex-patriots living on Crete. The membership is mostly from Northern Europe, for example, Germany, Belgium, France, Scandinavia and the UK, although there are some Greek members. They meet regularly for coffee and meals to raise money for charity. Their website also has helpful information for people who have moved, or are considering moving, to Crete. We were invited to their monthly coffee morning, which took place during our stay, but were unable to make it due to spending hours in the bank!

One of the members was very knowledgeable about the history of Rethymnon and spent a whole day giving us a tour. He explained a lot of interesting facts we had not picked up on our previous visits. For example, one of the main shopping areas is Arkadiou Street. We did not know that, at one time, this was the promenade until a row of houses was built between it and the sea. He also gave us information about many of the historic buildings. We had lunch at a family run taverna in Souliou Street, which was near where The Melody Garden used to be.

In the afternoon, he took us to his favourite coffee shop in a square in the town. Robin remembered the square from a previous visit because there was once a carpenter's workshop there. He had stopped to speak to the carpenter; by means of mostly sign language Robin managed to say that he was also a carpenter. The Cretan carpenter held up his hand to show where he had lost two fingers. Robin held up his to show that he had managed to keep all his - only just I might add! Before leaving us for the evening, our new friend took us to another bar where local people gather for raki, olives and local cheese. It was a very interesting day.

On another occasion we drove down to Agia Galini on the south coast; another of our favourite places. It is a pretty little harbour, although not as picturesque as Rethymnon. The town slopes quite steeply down to the sea and the streets are mostly stepped. We walked along the seafront to the next bay and stopped for a snack. We ordered tzatziki and cheese pies to share, which the waiter assured us, were; 'Made fresh by Mama this morning.'

I recall one occasion when I said something silly that made Robin laugh. The phone was ringing in reception at the Kriti Beach Hotel. Knowing how much I hate the phone, Robin said, 'It's for you!'

I meant to reply, 'Bog off!'

It came out as, 'Go bogging!'

Robin thought that was hilarious. Every time, after that, if I said something he disagreed with, he would tell me to go bogging.

Even while we were sorting out tax numbers, a bank account and residents' permits, we managed to have a late afternoon swim, or bob about in my case, most days and went out for a nice meal in the evenings. Our hotel had its own beach where, if we took the hotel beach towels, we could use the sun-beds, shower and changing rooms free of charge. There was also waiter service for drinks and snacks.

On one occasion we had a late afternoon swim. Robin used the changing room to get out of his wet swimming trunks. Then it came to my turn. I had my beach bag with towel, sunscreen, Kindle and beach mat. The only problem was, where was my underwear? I had left it behind in the hotel room. I had to go back to the hotel wearing only my sarong and matching bandeau top. Robin found this very funny but I was just praying there was not a sudden gust of wind!

In the evenings, we both liked to have a shower and dress up a bit to go out for a meal. Robin was a smart man and liked to change out of his daytime shorts and T-shirt into a pair of lightweight trousers and a short sleeved shirt. Part of the fun of the holiday for me was doing my hair and make-up, putting on jewellery and changing into a long dress.

We would then go down to the hotel bar for cocktails before going out to eat. I nearly always got a compliment from the barman. On occasion, if we had not been plied with too much raki after our meal, we would return for a nightcap. Of course, we realised things would be different when we were living on Crete but were determined to make the most of our last visit as tourists.

We finally managed to find an apartment to rent towards the end of the second week. That meant we had everything in place to apply for our residents' permits. Before leaving the UK, we had had passport photos taken but were told these may not be suitable for our residents' permits. We decided to play safe and have another set taken, explaining to the photographer what they were needed for. At the time I was wearing an off-the-shoulder dress so I look like I am naked in my photos!

We arranged to meet the lawyer at the police station. Once again, we arrived very early and the lawyer was running late. The police station is situated in a pleasant square with trees and fountains in the middle. On one side are a number of tavernas where local people have coffee in the mornings and wine and meze in the evenings. We had a coffee but still had plenty of time to spare. To occupy the rest of our time we had a short walk and discovered a small park and memorial to the Australian soldiers of World War II. It was interesting to read about the special relationship between Greece and Australia and the number of Greek people who emigrated to Australia after the war.

Obtaining our residents' permits was far more straightforward than we anticipated, although it amused Robin that they were processed by the Department for Aliens. He commented that we had arrived via EasyJet – not the Starship Enterprise! The police officer said they would be ready to collect in about ten days and they would notify us. This presented something of a problem. It was Friday and we were due to go home on Sunday. I asked the lawyer if she could collect them for us and she said she could but we would need to execute powers of attorney.

We accompanied her back to her office where she drew up the documents at no extra charge. They had to be signed in front of a properly authorised official. Normally this would be done at the KEP office (the Greek equivalent of our Citizens' Advice Bureau) but it was Friday afternoon and the office was closed. The other option was to take them to the police station.

The lawyer was also about to close for the weekend. She advised us to get to the police station straight away. If she was gone by the time we got back, we could leave the documents at the cake shop next door, where they often took in post for her. She said the smell of the sweets and cakes wafting up to her office was often very tempting.

Luckily for us, the staff at the police station spoke good English and were very helpful. We got the documents duly signed and properly witnessed in no time. I had put them in an envelope addressed to the lawyer and we were just about to go into the cake shop when I heard someone shout, 'Mrs Marilyn!' We had just caught our lawyer as she was leaving the office. When we explained that we would be moving to Crete permanently in November, she agreed to collect them and keep them in her safe until we returned.

Now everything was in place, we could relax. We met our friend from The Melody Garden and his partner at one of the tavernas near the police station for wine and meze. Robin, in particular, enjoyed this as it was a typical Cretan setting and the food was local, not designed for tourists.

On our last day we drove eastwards along the cost and spent the day in Panormo, a small fishing village. I recall asking for a small beer and ending up with a litre! Robin couldn't help me out because he was driving; it took me ages and Robin got through several Fantas before I finished it. We did a bit of last-minute shopping on our return. I bought myself a black bikini – I expected to need several when we were living here. I tried it on in the shop and remember Robin saying, 'That looks really good,' and that was after two weeks of wining and dining!

At the same time I bought a notebook and started making lists. One was for what we would need to bring with us. Then there was a list of friends and family I would need to give our new address. Finally, I made a note of all the utility companies and other organisations I would need to inform.

For our last evening, we had champagne in the hotel bar to celebrate our forthcoming move. We sat outside overlooking the sea and clinked glasses. Robin suddenly looked up at me and said, 'I do love you.'

We walked along to the restaurant belonging to the friend who took us to the bank. He had already offered to cook us some special fish and he had not exaggerated. Thankfully, we did not order a starter. He brought out an enormous platter containing a whole lobster, sea bass, prawns and mussels. Other diners looked on in amazement. By this time he knew which wine we liked so this was served immediately. It was a lovely evening made even better by the knowledge that we would shortly be returning – for good!

He even kindly offered to keep our luggage in his store-room until our return.

'There's no point in taking it home with you only to bring it back again in November,' he said, 'I have to pay rent for the restaurant even when it is closed in the winter, so you may as well leave it here.'

We had a late morning flight home on Sunday so had time

for breakfast at the hotel. This was just as well. On arrival at the airport we were met with a sea of people. In all the years we had been visiting Crete, we had never seen such queues at check-in. Someone told us that there had been an incident of some kind at Chania airport and some of the flights had been diverted to Heraklion. As flights became due for boarding, the flight numbers were being called out allowing passengers to go to the front of the queue so as not to miss their flights. Thankfully we managed to catch ours and it was only slightly delayed.

Chapter 5 – Looking for accommodation

As I mentioned previously, I had not had much success finding accommodation online before our return visit. I had seen a couple of long-term holiday lets, rented out by the month, that looked promising but it was too early to think about booking either of them. The plan was to have a look around once we arrived. However, by that time, they were no longer on the website.

We tried looking in the real estate agents' offices but the only rental accommodations available were villas that were outside our budget. They were also in villages and we did not want to live in a village. Everything in the town seemed to be rented out as Airbnb in the summer and student accommodation in the winter.

Our friend from the seafood restaurant suggested we try an apartment hotel. The rooms would be fairly small but they would have cooking facilities and were well within our budget. It would be an ideal temporary solution. He said he knew the owner of one and would get in touch with him for us. That sounded promising so we were able to relax for a couple of days, at least on that score - we were still sorting out tax numbers and a bank account. At that time, we planned to put our belongings into storage until we could sell our house in the UK and buy a property on Crete.

When we later went to the restaurant for a meal, the news was not good. The whole hotel was let out to students. Our friend did, however, suggest another hotel that we could try.

'I'm sorry, I can't come with you,' he said, 'I have a business to run.'

'We quite understand,' I replied, 'You have been more than helpful already.'

The next day we went to the hotel he suggested but the reception was closed. There was a phone number on the door so I wrote it down. When we stopped for a drink and lunch-time snack, I tried the number but could only get a recorded message in Greek. I repeated this several times with the same result. Staying in an ordinary hotel was not really an option because it would be too expensive and most of them would be closing for the winter in a few weeks anyway. Things were not looking good. We did not want to get everything else in place and then fall at the last hurdle.

That evening we went to the Melody Garden and the manager offered to get in touch with his real estate friend again. We were not keen but did not want to offend him so we agreed to meet. This time we said to each other that we would not be put under pressure. At that stage we could not afford to buy in any event, because our house in the UK was not even on the market. Luckily for us, it was pouring with rain on the evening we had agreed to meet the real estate agent, so we had a legitimate reason to cancel without offending anyone.

We had gone to the Globe, another of our favourites, for a lunchtime snack when it started raining. We sat there as long as we could but it got to the point where we did not want any more to eat or drink.

'We can't sit here any longer taking up seats without ordering anything else,' said Robin.

'Yes, I think we will just have to get wet,' I replied.

And get wet we certainly did! It was not far to our hotel but the rain was coming down hard turning the footpath into a river.

I texted our friend to say we could not make it because of the rain and he quite understood. That evening we ate at a restaurant close to the hotel because we did not want another soaking. As is typical of Crete, by the next day everything had dried up and the sun was shining again.

Our friend from the Melody Garden mentioned that his girlfriend had recently inherited an apartment we might be interested in. We arranged to meet at the shop where she worked early one day so that we could go and view the apartment before she opened up the shop. We were pre-warned that building work was being undertaken because there had been a leak from the roof and the previous tenants had taken a hammer to the fitted wardrobes.

The apartment was a building site but Robin was in the trade so he could see the potential. He was heartbroken to see the vandalism to the fitted wardrobes. What sold it to me was the beautiful fireplace. I could just imagine our Christmas tree standing in it. It had two large bedrooms and a smaller one, a huge kitchen cum living area and a good sized bathroom. Another selling point was the two large storage cupboards. Everything was close by, a butcher and a greengrocer right opposite with shops selling fresh fish and a supermarket just down the road. It was also within easy walking distance from the town. The view over the sea to the Fortezza, which is flood-lit at night, was beautiful.

Our friends ordered in coffee for us and we stayed for a while chatting to them and the builder. We did not have to think about it but said right away that we would take it. There was not very much furniture in the flat but the agreement was that it would be rented furnished because we could only bring a few things from the UK with us.

Later in the week we went to see the owner to let her know we were going to move into the flat in November. That is a day I will never forget! We arrived at about 4 p.m. Then we adjourned to the taverna opposite where she could keep an eye on the shop for potential customers. Wine and meze were ordered and we sat to drink and chat. To my surprise a cat jumped onto my lap. I am not really a cat person, I prefer dogs, but she made herself at home. I was told she was a very special cat and was not friendly with everyone. The fact that she had come to me was taken as a sign that we were destined to come to Crete.

Our friend had to go to work at the Melody Garden so he left us chatting, drinking wine and eating meze, which we continued to do all evening! When he came back to take his girlfriend home after closing the restaurant, he said in amazement, 'What? Are you still here?'

We often talk about that day even now. It was a lovely evening and we felt welcomed and so relieved we had found somewhere to rent.

On the following day we went back to the area of the apartment. We had a look round and found where everything was. The apartment was also close to the bus station and a taxi rank so all the facilities we could possibly want were close at hand. There is a taverna just across the road and we decided to stop there to share a half litre of wine. We sat by the sea and looked across the bay towards the Fortezza. Robin was so excited he told the waiter we would be moving to Crete in November.

Back in the UK I used to visit the gym three evenings a week because I spent all day sitting behind a desk. While we were sipping our wine, we noticed a fitness centre just a few hundred yards away.

'Everything is falling into place,' said Robin, 'We are meant to live here.'

It certainly seemed meant to be. When we paid our bill before leaving the hotel, Robin told the receptionist we had found an apartment and were coming back to live on Crete. She said,

'You were really lucky, it took me seven months to find my apartment and I was looking through the local papers every week.'

Chapter 6 – The move

I must admit that my first thought when we arrived home was, *what have we done?* We had just committed ourselves to leaving everything that was familiar and moving to a different country, over 1,000 miles away. One of the most difficult things I had to do was give in my notice. I enjoyed my job and was not really ready to leave it, but I knew if we did not make the move then, we would never do it. How right I was and how glad I am that we did it.

My boss and I worked well together so he was genuinely upset when I told him I was leaving. He did say he was not unduly surprised. Things were not going the way he and I had hoped with the department. I had given some hints as to why we were returning to Crete for a second visit that year.

Once I had handed in my notice, I was able to tell my colleagues and they were all really excited for me. Some of them had been to Greek islands for holidays and one man was actually Greek. He started teaching me a few Greek words. We discussed what I might be able to do work-wise once I got there. Someone suggested I could be a tour guide while another thought I could work behind the bar in a taverna.

Robin said, 'If all else fails, we can open a tea shop for English tourists. It's hard to get a decent cup of tea over there.'

Another difficult thing to do was to tell our family. Although we had been talking about moving to Crete for a number of years, it still came as something of a shock. Our daughter,

Karen, said, 'You have been saying you were going to Crete for years, I never thought you would really do it.'

I replied, 'We had to wait until I was eligible for the state pension because we will only have our pensions to live on when we first move there.'

Our granddaughter, Karen's daughter Zoe, lives and works on the Isle of Wight. As luck would have it, she was due for a visit the following weekend, so we arranged to meet at Karen's flat for a meal on the Saturday and to stay overnight.

The weekend was not a success because Zoe was upset at the prospect of us moving and worried about Karen being left alone with our grandson, Harvey, who has autism. She need not have worried. Karen's boyfriend, Paul, is a carer for his disabled brother and lives in the same block of flats. He would do anything for Karen and Harvey. Harvey loves him and his brother. We always called Paul and Keith 'the boys' and knew Karen and Harvey were being left in good hands.

If I thought handing in my notice and telling the family would be the hardest things to do, I was wrong! We had lived in our house for thirty three-years so it is not difficult to imagine the amount of rubbish we had managed to accumulate during that time. That was without even thinking about Robin's workshop at the end of the garden.

The first thing we had to do was to find international removers before we could decide what to take with us. Even though we knew there would be a bed in the apartment and there were fitted wardrobes in all three bedrooms, for some reason Robin wanted to take the bed and matching chest of drawers from our bedroom. Apart from that, there were a couple of items that had sentimental value such as my grandfather's clock and my grandmother's gate-leg table. Because Robin was a very keen amateur chef, he planned to entertain the friends we made on Crete. For this purpose, he wanted to take all our cutlery, crockery and glassware.

Robin also had to wind up his business. He loved his job and I could never imagine him not doing some form of woodwork. Clearly, he could not take all his tools with him. He had to sell the larger items, such as his bench saw, but gradually started to pack up his hand tools for the journey. He also had to call in a clearance company to deal with all the off cuts of wood, wood shavings and sawdust.

Sorting through the rubbish was a nightmare. There were a lot of things I really did not want to part with but we had to be sensible. They were just things, I tried to tell myself, it is people that matter and Robin and I would be together, that was what was important. Because he was self-employed, Robin had to keep all his accounts and vouchers for a set number of years in case HMRC needed to check them. A few years previously, I had been self-employed for a while so the same applied to me. We had to dispose of all the papers that went back before the set date.

When the children left home, we converted the small bedroom into a walk in wardrobe cum office. As well as our tax documents we had accumulated a lot of other paperwork that was no longer required. I had even kept all my notes and textbooks from when I had studied law, over twenty years previously! Most of the papers were confidential documents but the shredder just could not handle them all. In the end, Robin had to burn them in the garden.

'I just hope none of the neighbours complain to the

council,' he said, 'this is a smokeless zone; we aren't supposed to have bonfires!'

Once we had decided what to take with us, we obtained a quote from the international removers, which was eye watering. However, this did include their operatives doing all the packing. Not only could we not face doing this ourselves, but we took the view they were the experts and the items were more likely to arrive intact if they packed them.

The next few weeks were something of a sentimental journey. When Karen found out that we were not taking our dining table and chairs, she asked if she could have them.

'They are part of our childhood,' she said, 'I can remember Christmas dinners with the grandparents sitting round that table.'

It was also larger than hers. When Robin, Zoe, Karen and I with Paul and his brother, Keith, all got together for dinner, it was a bit of a squash. That was without Harvey because he did not sit at table with us at that time due to his autism, although he has made great strides since then

I continued to commute to London each day to work out my notice. As I began to tell work associates outside the business that I was leaving, they said they would miss working with me but wished me well. The only thing that irritated me was people telling me to enjoy my retirement. I was not retiring, just slowing down a bit! We had a hectic lifestyle and never seemed to have much time for each other. This move would give us the opportunity to spend more time together.

Because we were always busy during the week, on Saturdays we ate out. We had a few restaurants we liked and would visit them on a rota basis. Within walking distance of home, we had four that we visited regularly, a Thai, Chinese, Persian and Italian. The staff at all of them knew us. In particular, in the Chinese Robin was always given a crème de menthe and I was given a brandy on the house after our meal. We had spoken to the owner of the Italian often about moving to Crete so he was not surprised but said he would miss us. When eating in a restaurant Robin always wanted to sit with his back to the wall, facing into the restaurant. I used to joke that it was his MI5 training!

We booked the international removers for the week after I finished work. On my last day I was taken out to lunch by my colleagues. They also had a collection for me and I was presented with a card signed by everyone together with a Swarovski crystal pen and necklace. I had to give a speech. This was no big deal. As a chartered legal executive I was used to standing up in court and addressing the judge. On this occasion though, it was tinged with sadness because I enjoyed my job and would miss it. I had started on a three month contract but had gone on to become permanent staff. My boss joked that it was unusual for someone to be given a three month sentence and then go on to serve five years!

I worked in-house for a local authority. The following week, one of the partners in a firm of solicitors I worked closely with invited me out to lunch. As I was no longer an employee of the local authority he was able to do this without fear of any accusations of bribery. He and one of his fellow partners took me to a very nice restaurant. We had a lovely lunch and, again, I felt sad that I was leaving all these nice people behind.

The next task, of course, was sorting out our clothes. I have to admit, we both loved our clothes. Robin vehemently denied he had a feminine side, but I believed this was his love of clothes. Of course, he was fairly tall and slim with broad shoulders so he carried them off well. He wore a morning suit with panache at our younger daughter Nicky's wedding and looked handsome in a dinner jacket. Even wearing white tie and tails for investitures with the Order of St John did not make him feel uncomfortable. He wore the clothes, not the other way round.

He decided he would not need all his suits on Crete so kept only a couple of lightweight ones and his black one for funerals. I decided I would not need any of my work suits so I just kept one for any formal occasions and a black trouser suit for funerals. We filled the clothes bank at the nearby leisure centre so had to drive into town to continue filling the one in Waitrose's car park! I had to remember to keep enough clothes back from the removers to last us until our goods arrived on Crete.

At the time Karen's boyfriend drove a van for a furniture store and he was able to borrow it to collect the table and chairs and also our small chest freezer which Karen asked if she could have. She was always keen to have a freezer full of food so that, if she was short of money one week, she and Harvey would not go hungry. We passed our microwave and satnav to the boys.

We gave away everything we could. To mark the end of the working week, Robin always cooked a special meal on Fridays, usually fish. This was the only day of the week when we had a starter at home and we would open a nice bottle of wine. We would set the dining table and eat by candle light. On all other days we would sit on high stools at the kitchen counter to eat, so the loss of the dining table was not felt too keenly.

The removers were very efficient and packed our things in less than a day. When Robin was working in his workshop, he often went to a cafe round the corner for a snack at lunchtime. We had not had any breakfast so we left them to it and went for bacon sandwiches and a cup of tea (or coffee in my case). Because our bedroom furniture had been packed to go to Crete, we had to move into the spare bedroom for the few more days before we left. We had only slept in there before when Robin was decorating our bedroom so it seemed strange and brought home to me the fact that we were really going to move.

I spent a lot of time during the last days working on the laptop. There were a number of charities we donated to that I had to inform we could no longer support. On top of this, there were so many organisations we had to notify, such as HMRC, the local authority, our GP, utility companies, etc. Robin sold his van and our car to a work associate who agreed we could keep the car until our last day before leaving the UK, so we still had a means of transport.

When I was sorting out all our family photos, I came across a box full of letters my father sent to my mother when he was doing his National Service. Although I did not want to throw them away, I was reluctant to read them because they were too personal. I hit upon the idea of contacting the Imperial War Museum. To my delight, they said they would make a valuable addition to their archive because they gave a personal insight into the time of the Cold War. Students of the history of that era would find them of interest.

As we were now in November, I also had to think about Christmas. I had written out all our Christmas cards and put stamps on them to leave with Karen so that she could post them closer to Christmas. We belonged to a wine club and ordered a dozen bottles of wine every couple of months. Instead of cancelling the last order, we decided to give it to Karen as a Christmas present.

Robin's grandmother was Jewish. His mother had not really followed any faith but because the Jewish faith follows the female line his sister, June, became interested in it. She and her husband, Ray, converted to the Reformed Synagogue. Hanukkah usually falls close to Christmas so my Christmas shopping also included buying Hanukkah presents. There are eight days to Hanukkah so we usually bought small presents for the first seven days and the main present for the last day. I had brought a couple of small souvenirs back from Crete in October but had my work cut out to buy, pack and post 16 Hanukkah presents before we left the UK!

We sent out change of address cards to everyone we thought might be interested. One day when I was working in the kitchen, there was a knock on the door. When I answered it a woman stood on the doorstep. 'Can I help you' I asked.

Then I realised it was my brother's former wife. We had always got on well and had kept in touch after the divorce. In fact, she invited Robin and me to her wedding when she re-married. I felt so embarrassed that I had not recognised her but I had not expected to see her. She explained that she was in the area for her job and decided to call in and say. 'Hello,' before we moved. She had a cup of tea with us and I was able to show her where we were going to live on Google Street View.

We were now rapidly approaching our last weekend in the UK. I was still going to the gym and Robin did our usual Friday evening meal. Although Robin worked in construction, he was not much of a beer drinker but he did like a pint occasionally at lunchtime on a Saturday. That day we went to our local for a snack because it would be the last opportunity. Robin had a pint and I had a glass of wine. We felt a bit sad to think that it would be a long time, if ever, before we would go there again. It would also be our last opportunity to go shopping in Surbiton.

Instead of going out to eat on the Saturday evening, Karen invited us to her flat for a meal. She said the boys wanted to see us before we left, to say goodbye. It would be a while before we would be able to return for a visit. It was a nice evening and the boys gave us our Christmas presents to take to Crete with us.

Usually when we went for a meal at Karen's flat, we stayed overnight so that we could have a couple of glasses of wine and not have to worry about driving home. Karen did not own a car but had a designated parking space for our car registration number. We stayed for breakfast and then went home because we still had a few things to do.

As well as our usual Italian restaurant, there is another one in Surbiton that we liked very much but it was rather expensive so we reserved it for special occasions. Because this was our last weekend before the move, we decided it was a special occasion and had a late lunch/early dinner there. I cannot remember exactly what we had. I know we started with bread and olives and think we probably had steak for main course. The dessert remains a mystery! I do recall we had grappa after the meal, which is the closest we could get to raki.

Time was now really running out. I had my last body-combat class at the gym on Monday and then cancelled my membership. I did most of the packing on Monday because, the next day, we had a house clearance company coming in to remove the remaining furniture and other items we were not taking with us.

When my mother died, we had a house clearance company to empty her flat. They were brilliant. They also had a shop and anything that was saleable went into the shop. I expected this company to be the same but I was sadly disappointed. When Robin realised that they were simply clearing everything out and taking it to the tip, he took me out of the way to the cafe round the corner for a snack. When we got back I just sat in the car. I was almost in tears.

'They are not house clearers, they are house wreckers,' I said.

Just because we could not take everything with us, did not mean we did not care about things that had been part of our life over the last thirty-three years.

Once they had gone, we had to go in to clean up. We were not taking the vacuum cleaner with us, so we vacuumed all the carpets and it broke down just as we finished. It sounds silly, but the house seemed lonely without any furniture in it. It seemed strange to see it empty after we had lived there for so long. Robin reminded me that we were starting out on a new adventure.

The final job was to take our car to the colleague of Robin's who had bought it. He had agreed to give us a lift back to Karen's flat where we were staying the night. We almost forgot that we had personal items in the glove compartment and a folding umbrella in the door pocket. We arrived just as Karen was meeting Harvey's minibus from school. He seemed really grown-up when he shook hands with Robin's colleague.

Karen cooked us steak and kidney pie and mash, saying she thought we would like a last good old English meal before we went off to eat Greek food. Normally, we had a habit of only drinking alcohol at weekends but, because this was a special occasion and our last evening as UK residents, we shared a bottle of wine. Then Robin said, 'I had better arrange a cab to take us to the airport tomorrow.'

'Aren't we driving to the airport?' I asked without thinking.

'No, silly,' he replied, 'We don't have a car!'

Chapter 7 – The journey

Although we had paid for an extra suitcase, I still had trouble squeezing everything we needed to take into three suitcases. We had taken them to Karen's flat before we handed over the car. In addition, I also had to find space for our Christmas presents from the boys, so we had to leave one or two things behind. Karen agreed to hold onto them until we could collect them.

It was something of an emotional parting when we left for Gatwick the next day. Karen gave us a hug and told us to come back soon for a visit. Direct flights to Crete had finished at the end of October so the first leg of our journey was to Athens. It was a bittersweet journey to Gatwick airport. We had done the same journey so many times but it seemed strange to pass the familiar landmarks and realise this would no longer be home. It was the end of an era.

Problems occurred at bag drop. We had paid for the extra case and I had been careful to make sure each case was within the weight limit, although only just! This had necessitated leaving behind some items we would have preferred to bring with us. For some reason, the automatic bag drop machine weighed one of our cases at well over the weight limit. Even with the assistance of one of the ground crew, we were not able to have it re-weighed. The cheapest option turned out to be to pay for another extra case rather than excess baggage. How annoying! We could have brought all the things we had to leave behind.

In fact, that probably would not have been a good idea. Robin was usually fairly easygoing but was beginning to get slightly grumpy at having to manoeuvre three cases.

I had decided it would be best to stay overnight at an airport hotel in Athens and continue our journey to Crete the next day. That way we would not have the added stress of trying to make a connection, especially if our first flight was delayed. We had a room at the Sofitel which was quite comfortable. It was a pleasant surprise to discover that the hotel was only 50 metres from the airport, so we only had a short distance to wheel our three cases. The receptionist was surprised to see a Greek address on our check in form, especially as I had booked using our UK address.

The room was quite small but comfortable. After settling in, we went down to the bar and decided to start our adventure in Greek style. Although the flight from Gatwick to Athens is only just over three hours, it felt like we had been travelling all day. In addition to the flight, there was the usual waiting about at baggage reclaim once we had gone through security. As a result, we were too tired to go into the restaurant for a meal and decided to eat in the bar. There was quite a good selection of bar snacks and we went for the meze plate and a bottle of Greek wine. We felt a bit like Nomads with no fixed abode. Although we no longer lived in the UK, we had yet to take up residence in Greece.

While sitting in the bar having our supper there was a most spectacular thunderstorm. The thunder crashed and lightening backlit the mountains. Despite the force of the storm, we sat spellbound and found it a romantic experience. I have never been afraid of thunderstorms but we were both glad we were not flying that night. I took a picture of Robin with his glass of wine to send to Karen to let her know we had arrived in Athens safely.

The flight the next day was in the afternoon, so we had plenty of time to have a leisurely breakfast and try to repack the cases, thankfully for the last time. I was more than a little worried when we saw the sniffer dogs at the airport. The presents from the boys were chocolate and I thought the dogs might sniff them out and it would look like we were transporting drugs! Fortunately the dogs were well trained and not interested in chocolate. There was no issue with excess baggage at Athens airport so the flight to Chania passed without incident apart from a bit of turbulence.

This was the first time we had flown into Chania; previously we had always flown to Heraklion. Chania is a smaller airport but it is much cleaner and, of course, less busy. We decided that we would always use Chania in the future as it is much nicer. We had arranged to collect a hire car at the airport which we would keep for a couple of days and then return to the office in Rethymnon. We would not only need it for the journey from the airport but also to collect our other suitcases from our friend's restaurant.

We were not familiar with the route from Chania Airport to Rethymnon. In spite of our intention to avoid the town centre, we ended up there at least twice. On one occasion we found ourselves on the National Road heading in the wrong direction. A number of detours were made and we had to stop and ask for directions before we found our way to the National Road, heading for Rethymnon!

Our landlady and her partner were waiting for us at the

apartment. We were told that it is customary for travellers to be welcomed home with food and wine. They had a box of Retsina waiting in the fridge along with some beers. There were also cheese pies and spinach pies, both local delicacies, which we nibbled on as we were shown round. The apartment looked completely different from when we had last seen it. It was newly decorated and the fitted wardrobes had been repaired. Of course it was his trade, so Robin was often critical if he saw poor workmanship but he commented that the builder had made a good job of the renovations. The poor builder was still there in the evening putting in the finishing touches, such as hanging curtains.

Later, our friends ordered takeaway and we sat on the balcony drinking Retsina and eating gyros, souvlaki and Greek salad. The builder joined us and neighbours dropped by to say hello and share a glass of wine. We really felt welcomed. Imagine sitting on the balcony on a November evening and not being freezing cold!

Chapter 8 – Settling in

Well, we had done it! Now we were officially Crete residents. Our first few days were taken up with finding our way around. Although we knew Rethymnon fairly well from our holidays, living here was a different matter. The first thing I needed to do was to set up Wi-Fi. On our first attempt we could not find the shop we were recommended to. A visit to our landlady's shop, accompanied by wine and meze, put us on the right track and we managed to get it set up the next day.

It had been our intention to drive to the restaurant where our cases were stored on the day after our arrival but, having had a couple of glasses of wine with our friends, we had to put it off. The hire car needed to be returned the next morning so we would not be able to drive there. Robin said it was not a problem because the suitcases had wheels; it was not as if we had to carry them.

The restaurant was closed for the winter so our friend had told us to go to his wife's shop. He was out of the country at the time, so his wife took Robin to collect the suitcases while I stayed in the shop, keeping my fingers crossed no customers came in! It seemed a long way wheeling the two cases home but we eventually got them back. Of course, they were full of dirty laundry but there were a couple of items we needed. The laundry I did a bit at a time to put away ready for the following summer.

Until our bedroom furniture arrived, we slept in the front

bedroom. Next to it in the hallway, there is an alcove which Robin decided would be the ideal place to hang my grandfather's clock. For the first couple of days I had a habit of walking into the alcove in mistake for the door to the living room!

The furniture for the apartment had been ordered well in advance but only the bed had arrived in time. Our landlady had helped us out by providing some essentials to keep us going until our belongings arrived from the UK; such as cutlery, crockery and even soap in the bathroom. Curtains were up at the windows and she had brought bedding and a blanket in case we were cold.

It was a bit like camping out because we only had the metal tables from the balcony, folding chairs and a couple of armchairs that were already in the apartment. We did not mind; it was all part of the adventure. There were a few teething problems with the cooker – it kept shorting out the electricity! The first meal Robin 'cooked' for me was cheese pie from the bakery and salad. It was enjoyable all the same and the problem was soon resolved.

We had put our names down for lunch with the CIC on the following Sunday, only three days after our arrival. We took a taxi there because we had not sorted out a bus timetable and Robin was never a fan of public transport anyway. At first, we felt a little awkward because we had only met one of the members of the CIC before. Following Robin's custom of arriving everywhere early, we ended up having a drink in the bar because we were at the restaurant before most of the others. Once we sat down for the meal, we got chatting to the couple sitting opposite us and found we had a lot in common. Adrienne and Nick turned out to be very good friends. They even gave us a lift home. I recall Robin having a little too much raki, falling out of the back of their car and stubbing is toe on the kerb. He still had a black toenail months later.

After all the stress and excitement of the move and the journey, we decided to take things easy on the Monday and just settle in. Fate had other ideas. Following his builder's curiosity, Robin had been up on the roof to have a look round. He wanted to show me the solar power for the water heating and also the view over the sea and the Fortezza.

'Just close the door,' he said, 'you can turn the knob to get back in.'

Of course, we could not. Once the door was closed it was locked. So there we were, no money, no phones, everything was locked inside the apartment.

That turned out to be a very stressful day. We could not call the owner because both our phones were locked in the apartment. Her shop was closed when we walked down to it. Although we asked at the taverna opposite, they had no contact details for her, so could not call her for us. We could not check into a hotel because all our money and cards were locked in the apartment. What were we to do? Luckily for us, Robin was of a practical frame of mind. There was a fair amount of rubbish lying around that the builder had not had time to clear away. Robin found a thin piece of metal he was able to slide down the doorframe to click the lock open. I have never been so pleased to see the inside of the apartment either before or since!

Robin was concerned at the ease with which he broke into the apartment. As soon as his tools arrived from the UK, he spent a morning making a frame to go over the side of the doorframe where the locks were. Thus, he ensured no-one else could get in using the same method. He probably need not have worried. The Cretans are basically honest. We saw people go to the WC in restaurants leaving their phones on the table. Robin commented more than once about how builders left their tools in the open back of pick-up trucks. This particularly amazed him, after having all his tools stolen from a locked van on three separate occasions in the UK.

Later that week we both went to the hairdresser who, fortunately for us, spoke reasonable English. Robin had his hair cut first and left saying he would meet me at home. She did a very good job for both of us and charged less than half of what I regularly paid in the UK. When I got home, Robin had started to organise the kitchen to his liking. Even though our belongings had not yet arrived from the UK, it was starting to feel like home.

Later that week the rest of the furniture arrived. It was all in flat pack so Robin and our landlady's partner struggled to put it together with a couple of small screwdrivers. Then Robin remembered the builder had left his battery drill in the spare bedroom and had not yet been back to collect it. The battery lasted just long enough for Robin to put the furniture together. He looked so at home with a battery drill in his hands.

We were told our goods from the UK would take about three weeks to arrive. Robin's main concern was to get the tree and decorations in time for Christmas. Of course, we were getting fed up with wearing the same clothes all the time and were eagerly anticipating the arrival of the rest of them!

Just over two weeks from our move, we were going for a walk when Robin's phone rang. It was a message to say that several pallets of boxes were on their way from Heraklion. That cut our walk short. I kept the removal men supplied with cold water during their numerous journeys up the stairs with the boxes, which seemed to fill the apartment. Robin and I spent the rest of the day unpacking.

Several of the boxes went into the large cupboards for attention at a later date. There were only a couple of minor breakages which Robin was able to repair. It was Robin himself who managed to break a couple of glasses while unpacking. Although the bed that came with the apartment was comfortable, it was nice to have our own bedroom furniture. It made the apartment feel more like home.

I unpacked the clothes and put them away in the various fitted wardrobes. The summer clothes went in the spare room and winter clothes went in our bedroom. Holiday clothes went in the small bedroom that we had already decided would be my sewing room. Robin unpacked a lot of the glassware and crockery so he could set up the kitchen. He also decided which pictures we would put on the wall.

In our house in Surbiton, we had a large blank wall which we had covered with family photos. There are six generations, my great-grandparents, our grandparents, our parents, us, our children and grandchildren. Robin said, 'It's not our flat, so we can't go banging holes in the wall. We can only put pictures up where there are already nails.'

He chose a collage of family pictures our granddaughter had put together as a present for us several years ago. He insisted on the photo taken on my graduation as a Fellow of the Chartered Institute of Legal Executives, a picture of each of our family members and, of course, our wedding photo. When we first visited Greece in 1998 staying on Rhodes, we had a chalk sketch made of us. It has survived for over 20 years and it holds pride of place over the fireplace. Robin even managed to find places for photos of our dogs over the years and one of us in our cloaks and regalia for the Order of St John.

He had a good eye for where things would fit. I had a display cabinet that had been a present from a grateful client and I had filled it with treasures from holidays and small presents from family. There was an alcove in the living room where he said it would fit perfectly, and it did! The same went for the other alcove in the hallway that now houses my grandfather's clock, along with hats we brought back from Vietnam and Mexico.

When we moved in, the apartment had an old washing machine. It worked perfectly well; I had used it many times before our belongings arrived because we had a limited number of clothes with us. However, our landlady wanted to get us a new one. We went to the CIC coffee morning on the first Monday in December. While we were there, Robin received a phone call to say the new one would be arriving the following day.

We had not realised it but that day was St Barbara's Day. St Barbara is the patron saint of Rethymnon so it was a public holiday. We had no idea where the taverna hosting the coffee morning was so we took a cab. It turned out to be within reasonable walking distance. We therefore decided to walk back and luckily found a supermarket that was open so we could get a few essentials.

The washing machine duly arrived, was plumbed in and the old one taken away. The next time I did some washing, the machine made a horrible grinding noise which we thought could not possibly be right. We called our landlady who, in turn, called the manufacturer. I had to take a photo of the machine and email it to them. A repair man arrived and replaced a part. The machine still made the horrible nose. Our landlady wanted it replaced with a new one, but the manufacturer insisted on repairing this one.

We became intimately acquainted with the local launderette, after being instructed in the use of the machines by students from the university! After several calls by our landlady, the repair man finally returned. He spoke quite good English. Robin kept trying to tell him, 'It keeps making a *graunching* noise.'

I am not sure he could recognise the word *graunching* but seemed to understand what Robin was trying to tell him. He told Robin afterwards, 'I have replaced its brains and its bottom, so it should work now.'

Fortunately, it did.

When packing our things for the move, my display cabinet and the bookcases were reduced back down to flat packs for easy transportation. On unpacking here on Crete, Robin was unable to find the screws and clips to put them back together. All the contents of my display cabinet were currently on a table in the bedroom. I was worried something would get broken. At our first CIC coffee morning, a lady told Robin where he could buy what he needed. It was a short walk down the road, so we went along there and Robin was delighted to find he could buy just what he wanted. In the UK he always had to buy a pack containing a certain number even if he only needed one or two. Of course, as soon as he had bought replacements, further unpacking revealed the originals!

Shortly after we moved in, we managed to break the toilet

seat. I think it was already on its last legs but, as we finished it off, Robin said we should pay to replace it. We went to see our landlady to ask where we could buy a new one. Her partner was there, it being winter so he was not working. He took Robin off to find a plumbing shop.

They seemed to be gone for ages. Apparently they had been all over town. Most of the shops were either closed or did not stock that particular type. He had remarked to Robin 'Doesn't anyone sit down to use the toilet in this town?'

They eventually found a shop where the owner agreed to order one in for the next day. When we returned the next day, it had not arrived. Again, the owner left us minding the shop while he went off in his car to fetch it!

Robin was concerned that there was a smell of drains in the bathroom. I could not smell it myself but it bothered him. I mentioned that we had brought a Febreze air freshener with us from the UK. He said, 'Oh that was empty so I threw it.'

Of course he meant he threw it away, But I could not help laughing as I pictured him opening the bathroom window and pitching it down the street! Not to be deterred, he bought an air freshener with a battery that lets out bursts of fragrance at set intervals. Until I got used to it, it startled me every time it sprayed. It clearly had the same effect on Robin because I remember him saying one day, 'There's a little elf in the bathroom that keeps coughing and making me jump!'

I tend to suffer from migraine and on the second Saturday in December I succumbed to a particularly unpleasant one. Robin had to go to the supermarket on his own. On his return he came to see me to ask if I needed anything. He was thrilled to find that he had won a ten Euro cheque against the next shop.

He also proudly showed me a box of cereal saying, 'I got you some cereal; I know how you like your cereal.'

Not only had he taken the trouble to buy me cereal but had sought out the low calorie variety. He was always thoughtful like that.

When he got his Euro cheque, Robin was advised to apply for a bonus card. Not only would this add up points that could be redeemed against our shopping every so often, but entitled us to the discounts shown on various items throughout the store. Without a bonus card, these were not available. On our next visit, Robin told me to apply for it because people understood my English better. When we got home, he looked at it and said, 'I know it's close to Christmas, but they have put you down as *Merry-lyn*!

It was especially pleasant for Robin to be able to just pop across the road and buy fresh meat and produce almost every day. He said it was so much nicer than getting it all delivered from the supermarket and, of course, it was fresher. He would often go across the road and come back with a bag full of vegetables to make soup for lunch. Usually, he wanted me to go to the butcher with him because he said they did not understand his Lincolnshire accent.

On one occasion Robin went into town on his own and was tickled to be asked by some tourists, needing directions, if he spoke English. He did not let on that he was English, just said,

'Yes, I speak it very well!'

Of course, with his Jewish ancestry he was quite dark skinned so it was not surprising that people thought he was Greek.

One thing we did not have in the apartment was a television. It did not bother me but Robin liked certain TV shows. Being an enthusiastic amateur chef, his favourites were the TV chefs, especially the Hairy Bikers. While I was incapacitated with the migraine, I was delighted to see that he had started his sketching again. He had not done that for years. I had brought my knitting with me in the suitcase. We got into the habit of going for a walk every evening after dinner, but on returning, spent many a pleasant evening listening to the radio or CDs with Robin sketching and me knitting.

I finished a pullover for him that I had started before leaving the UK. He was really pleased with it. I can remember him trying it on and saying, 'You've made a good job of this; you can knit me another one in a different colour for next winter.'

Neither of us knew at the time that he would not see another winter.

Although it was winter, there were still several restaurants open so we continued our habit of eating out on Saturday evenings. Now we were more relaxed and did not have to get up early on Monday morning for the weekly commute, Robin liked to cook Sunday lunch at home and we would go out for a glass of wine in the evening. We often went to Galero in the centre of the Old Town next to the Rimondi fountain.

We got to know the waiter who works front of house, and a girl from Sweden, who works behind the bar. She was often pleased to chat with us when things were quiet. She said it helped the evening pass more quickly. I remember telling her one evening that I did not like tea, to which she replied, 'Are you sure you're English?'

There was a gallery above the bar with a piano, guitars and drums. Robin had to pass these to visit the WC and often threatened to bang on the bongos on the way back.

Robin's birthday was on 19 December and I always made sure that we did something special. Growing up, he often missed out because his birthday was so near Christmas. He would either get only a small present for his birthday or a joint Christmas and birthday present. I used to tell him he should have an official birthday in the summer, like the Queen. It was enough for Robin this year that he was finally living his dream. We did, however, go out for a meal. The weather was good so we were able to sit outside under an awning and the Christmas decorations added to the atmosphere.

It was always our tradition to make sure the Christmas decorations were up before Robin's birthday. Due to his artistic nature, it was always his job. This year he decorated the tree early in December. He was so excited about spending Christmas on Crete. To my disappointment, the Christmas tree would not fit in the fireplace. We put it on my grandmother's table nearby and in the fireplace we set up our crib scene. Robin made it extra special with lots of candles. His sister had sent us a parcel which arrived in plenty of time so we had presents under the tree. Everything was set for our first Christmas in our new home.

Chapter 9 – Christmas shopping

The CIC Christmas lunch in December was at Panormo, which is quite a distance from Rethymnon and we had no transport. It was also on the same day as the Friends of Animals Rethymnon Christmas lunch. Both of us were animal lovers and were keen to support this event, so we decided to forgo the CIC lunch in favour of the animal welfare one. I wanted to get a dog but Robin did not agree with keeping a dog in an apartment. He thought it should have a garden to run in. Greece does not have a good reputation for animal welfare so the animal rescue organisations need all the help they can get.

The lunch was held at the White Lady in Adelianos Kampos, which is a tourist village just outside Rethymnon. When driving from the airport at Heraklion, we usually turned off the National Road onto the old road into Rethymnon and had often passed it. We always thought it looked rather nice. The taverna caters for ex-patriots and we knew karaoke was on the programme. This was not really our thing so we did have some reservations. Adrienne and Nick were going as well. Adrienne is a retired vet so also has an interest in animal welfare and they have a handsome German Shepherd called Vito. I remember Nick showing us a photo of Vito covered in Christmas decorations. Nick thought once he started piling the decorations onto the sofa, Vito would move but Vito was staying put no matter what!

As it turned out, it was quite a good day. The karaoke singers could actually sing so it was entertaining and the food was good. It also gave us an opportunity to further our friendship with Adrienne and Nick, something I would come to be glad of. The high point of the afternoon for us was winning first prize in the raffle, which was a Christmas hamper. The taverna owners were thrilled for us. Robin made me go up and collect the prize and they took my photo holding the basket. It contained some chocolates; bottles of vodka, sherry and red wine; among other things, but it was only when we got home and found an envelope tucked in the basket, that we realised it included a voucher for a free turkey! When we told our landlady she said, 'The universe welcomes you.'

We certainly felt that we were meant to be on Crete and were set for a happy life here.

We stood the bottles of alcohol on the worktop in the kitchen. Nearby was a bottle of green Fairy liquid. I remember Robin saying, 'I'd better not come home tipsy, see that near the booze, and think it's crème de menthe!'

It took us a while to find the butcher's shop we had to collect the turkey from. There was a card with the voucher but the address was in Greek. We had a street map of Rethymnon but a lot of the streets do not have the names on them, or are not marked on the map. One branch of the butcher's chain was near to the post office and we asked in there. We were told it was down the road on the left but far away. Robin was all for giving up. He was not a great lover of turkey, which we had not had at home for years, and would have been quite happy with a nice piece of beef for Christmas lunch. I felt we should use the voucher when the butcher had been good enough to donate it free of charge.

Eventually, after walking from one side of Rethymnon to the other, we found the shop and arranged to collect our turkey on the Saturday before Christmas. We recalled afterwards that we had once stayed at a hotel on that side of town. The hotel website had optimistically stated that it was near the Fortezza and the Old Town! Robin decided we should stop for a coffee before making the walk back to our apartment. After spending most of his working life either kneeling down fitting skirting boards or climbing around on roofs, his knees were not as good as they used to be. Later, he was to find that living in Crete's healthier climate made his joints much more flexible. As we did not have a car, we ended up doing a lot of walking, which we both enjoyed.

As I mentioned earlier, I had managed to do most of our Christmas shopping before we left the UK but there were a few things left to do. Most of the family received vouchers but we had brought our food heaters for the table with us. Previously, we had always taken these to Karen at family occasions. Even though we would not be able to get back for Christmas, the boys would be round for Christmas lunch and she wanted to make it a special occasion. We decided we needed to buy her some replacements as an extra Christmas present. These were duly ordered online, along with Harvey's Christmas present, for delivery to Karen's address.

That only left each other. Although I suggested to Robin that we had each other and did not need Christmas presents, he was adamant that he had to buy me something. I had no idea what to buy Robin and he was the same with me. He wanted to buy me a watch but he had already bought me one for our

Ruby Wedding Anniversary earlier that year and I had several watches. Unknown to me, he had been into a shop selling sexy underwear but they told him they really needed to see me to get the size right. That would have done away with the surprise.

We also wanted to buy something for our landlady after she had done so much for us and brought us a lovely box of Greek Christmas biscuits. After looking all round town for a bouquet of flowers, we could only find artificial ones or pot plants. In the end we decided on a poinsettia. She was really pleased with it.

We hired a car with the intention of Christmas shopping in Chania. Unfortunately for us, that day was one of the few wet days we had that winter. By the time we arrived in Chania the rain was coming down in sheets. We parked near the harbour and the waves were crashing against the shore. Parts of the harbour were flooded so we could not walk round it. I took some photos to send to a former work colleague who loved storms and wild weather. It was certainly spectacular. The rain was coming down so hard we had trouble even seeing where we were going.

Instead of shopping, we ended up just having some lunch and then coming home. Determined to make a day of it, in spite of the weather, we took our time over lunch. Robin allowed himself a small beer and I had a glass of wine. I cannot remember what we had except that it included chips which were oven chips. That was a bit of a disappointment because one of the things we enjoyed about Crete was having proper fried chips. Everywhere in the UK now seems to serve oven chips, probably because they are easier to make and more healthy. They just do not taste the same. Apart from that, I remember the food being good. We were the only customers, so while having lunch we were chatting to the waitress. When she asked us where we were from, Robin proudly replied, 'Rethymnon!'

On our way back we did manage to find the British Supermarket at Litsarda. I did not envy Robin the drive through the mist and the rain up the narrow, winding hill roads. We drove past it the first time. Friends had referred to it as 'Green Gibble' but, in the rain, we could not see a sign. It turned out that what we thought was a pub 'The Ex Parrot' was the sign for the supermarket. It was of course, a play on words for ex-patriot.

I had brought mincemeat with me from the UK but discovered we could get it there. Every year I made my own mince pies. Robin always said mine were better than any we could buy in the shops because they were not so sweet and my pastry was lighter. We picked up a few things not readily available in the local supermarket such as pork pies and black pudding, as well as cranberry sauce for the turkey. It was surprising how much of the stock was also available in the local Greek supermarket but I suppose people get used to the well-known brands.

Christmas Eve was a Sunday that year. Most of the shops on Crete close on Sundays, especially in the winter, so we thought they would be closed on Christmas Eve. That left only 23 December for us to buy each other's presents. After we had collected our turkey and gone into town, it turned into another very wet day. I had no idea what to buy Robin so I ended up walking all around town getting wetter by the minute. I looked in various men's shops. Robin was young for his age, but these all seemed to cater for a much younger age group. I knew Robin would buy me something nice so I was getting really worried that I would not find something suitable. Eventually, I settled on a holder containing various olive oils, salts and vinegar (for his hobby of cooking) and a long sleeved polo shirt. Robin liked to wear polo shirts when dressing casually so I thought a long sleeved one would be ideal for the winter.

By this time I was thoroughly soaked. I had a raincoat with a hood but the rain had seeped through the seams. The same thing had happened with my boots. Robin had a coat with a hood but much preferred using an umbrella; I found them to be a nuisance. Robin had finished his shopping long before me and was home when I arrived. I remember saying, 'I couldn't be more wet if I had jumped in the sea!'

I was soaked through to my underwear. Robin told me to get straight into the shower while he made me a hot drink. At least I had Robin's Christmas present!

The annoying thing was that the shops were all open on Sunday, because it was Christmas Eve, and that day was dry and sunny!

Chapter 10 – Christmas

Robin and I were surprised to note both the similarities and differences in the way Christmas is celebrated on Crete. What we enjoyed about it most was the lack of the blatant commercialism that underlines the celebration in the UK. Decorations are not put up until the beginning of December, at the earliest in late November. When they do go up, the Old Town in particular is enchanting. I recall remarking to Robin that it was like fairyland.

I particularly remember walking through the car park near the Municipal Gardens one evening. I believe we were going to the post office, which stays open until 8 p.m. in Rethymnon. It was lovely to hear the Christmas songs and carols being played over the loudspeaker system. Many were in English but it did seem strange to hear some of the familiar carols being sung in Greek.

I had bought Robin a Christmas card before leaving the UK and brought it with me. Cretans do not really go in for greeting cards but there are some available in the bookshops. Robin went out and bought me a card. He could only get a plain one but he wrote inside, 'I fell in love with you years ago and it just gets stronger.'

I wrote in mine, 'I hope this will be the first of many happy Christmases in our new home.'

I still have both cards in Robin's memory box.

Lent is celebrated before both Easter and Christmas on

Crete. For the Christmas Season this starts on 15 November. Before this, the women of the household bake *Kourambiedes* and *Melamakorana* biscuits, but these are not traditionally eaten until after the end of Lent. We went to several tavernas where we were given the traditional Christmas biscuits to try, with our raki, after our meal. I recall one evening in December, our landlady called round to see how we were settling in and brought us a box of the Christmas biscuits beautifully done up with red ribbon. It seemed a shame to undo and eat them! At least I was able to reciprocate by giving her some mince pies.

We had brought two jars of mincemeat with us and I managed to get through both of them. Robin liked my home made mince pies so much; he could not get enough of them. When I commented how quickly he was getting through them, he would say, 'It wasn't me, it was that big mouse!'

The Christmas tree was first introduced to Greece in 1833 by the Bavarian King Otto. Until then, the traditional Greek decoration was a simple wooden boat. Both Christmas trees and illuminated wooden boats are a common feature of the decorations in the town. Seeing both traditions side by side added to the enchantment of our first Christmas on Crete. One of the first phrases in Greek we learned was *Καλά χριστούγεννα* (Happy Christmas) and we used it whenever we had the opportunity.

We had both become somewhat jaded by the commercialism of a UK Christmas but had been looking forward to celebrating it on Crete. In the lead up to Christmas, various events are put on in the square behind the former mosque. There are displays of Greek dancing, singing and various stalls and rides for children. I offered to buy Robin some candy-floss but he said, 'What with my beard? Can you imagine the mess I'd get in? I'd have to shave it off!'

I liked his beard, it suited him, and so I did not want him to shave it off.

Children of all ages are out early on Christmas Eve with their triangles to sing the Christmas *Kalanta* in the hope of earning a little extra pocket money; very much like our carol singing.

There is a Roman Catholic church in the Old Town. The Parish Priest serves a number of parishes so there is no Midnight Mass in Rethymnon. Christmas Eve mass takes place at 9 p.m. instead. Robin and I were used to attending midnight mass in the UK so we wanted to go along even though we were not Roman Catholics. It was something of an eye opener! The fact that the service was in Greek was not a problem. We were familiar with the mass having been high church Anglicans in the UK. What we found off-putting was that the local population treated it as a social occasion. People were walking in and out throughout the service. Children were running around and the two elderly ladies sitting in front of us, kept up a non-stop conversation throughout the service! Of course, most people would be attending Christmas services at the town's many Greek Orthodox churches.

We had bought a bottle of champagne to celebrate our first Christmas in our new home. After breakfast, Robin started preparing our Christmas lunch. He would spend hours poring over recipe books deciding what to cook and this was no exception. All the time we had been together, he had cooked Christmas lunch, apart from when we spent the time at my parent's home or stayed in a hotel. The turkey was so big; he had to cut the legs off to get it in the oven. These were put in the freezer to provide a Sunday lunch in the New Year.

Once lunch was on the go, it was time to open our presents. Robin decided we should have some champagne to accompany our present opening. I have a lovely photo of him standing by the fireplace with a glass in his hand. He had gone to so much trouble finding the right presents for me. I always liked the old fashioned idea of having a handbag to match my shoes. My green one was wearing out so he not only found me a green handbag, but made sure it was also real leather. I had admired some tassel earrings in town. Robin, being the generous man he was, did not buy me just one pair, but two. He said the shop assistant had told him, 'Your wife is a lucky girl.'

I replied, 'I know I am,' and kissed him.

We had some lovely presents from the family as well. Mine to Robin seemed meagre but he appeared to be pleased with them. He always got more pleasure from giving than receiving.

Robin did the cooking so it was my job to set the table. Although Robin was the artistic one, I always enjoyed making the table look nice. We had a red and gold Christmas table setting that had been a present from Robin's sister several years ago. I used this and set out some red glasses we had. Robin decided some tzatziki and a few crackers would be more than enough for a starter and arranged this nicely on plates with slices of cucumber. The table looked so lovely; I took a photo of it. After getting through the bottle of champagne while opening our presents, we could only manage one glass of wine each with lunch. Robin cooked the turkey to perfection. It was 'roasted' over a pan of white wine, which was later used to make the gravy, so was not dry at all.

Robin said he wanted a Christmas pudding and I had made a reasonable job of making one, although not all the usual ingredients were available. I had an old recipe for what was called Economical Christmas pudding, which all the family preferred because it was lighter than the traditional variety. I usually made brandy butter to accompany it but Robin was not keen and wanted custard. We had bought some custard powder on our visit to the British supermarket, so he got his custard.

Because of the two hour time difference, we did not call the family until after lunch. When we had spoken to them all we decided to go for a walk. One of our favourite walks was along by the sea, round the promontory where the Fortezza was situated, and into the town. It was a nice sunny day, not cold at all, and people were actually swimming. As we rounded the point by the Fortezza, the sun was starting to go down and it turned the snow pink on the top of Mount Psiloritis. It was a beautiful sight and really topped off our day.

We were surprised to note that some bars and restaurants were open on Christmas Day, although it is really a family occasion. We had enjoyed the day, but we did find it rather quiet, especially without a television. It was decided that the following year we would go to a restaurant for Christmas lunch. The traditional Christmas lunch on Crete is pork stew although turkey is now becoming more popular. Seared pieces of partially cooked pork are also offered as a late breakfast. A special bread is baked for Christmas Day known as Christopsomo, or Christ Bread. It is Boxing Day when families are more likely to eat out in the village tavernas. Of course it is not called Boxing Day on Crete, it is known as the second day of Christmas.

Chapter 11 – New Year

Now began the turkey marathon! As I mentioned previously, Robin was not a great turkey lover. In previous years we had had venison on occasion or duck but, more frequently, a goose on Christmas Day. We would also have a ham which Robin would boil in cider and then bake in the oven in a honey glaze. Whatever we decided to have for the main day, we always had cold meat, bubble & squeak and pickles on Boxing Day. Robin always said he enjoyed this more than the meal on Christmas Day.

This year was no exception. In addition to the turkey, we had bought a small gammon joint at the British supermarket. Cider is available in the local supermarket and, of course, honey is plentiful in Greece. So we had cold turkey and ham with bubble & squeak and pickles on Boxing Day. Robin also liked a fried egg with a runny yolk on his bubble & squeak. Some of the cooked meat had to go into the freezer but I recall that week we had turkey fajitas and I made a turkey and ham pie. Robin even made turkey burgers. It was a while before we could face turkey again!

Apart from a couple of years when we actually went to a hotel for Christmas, it was always a family occasion. By contrast, New Year was just for us. For the past few years we had booked a couple of nights in a hotel with a black tie dinner and dancing to see in the New Year. Robin had been a teenager in the rock 'n' roll era and was excellent at the jive. He taught me and we loved to dance. Often we even ended up with a round of applause! Due to the move, we had not managed to book anything this year. It was too soon for a visit back to the UK. I spent a lot of time on the internet but could not see anything suitable in the local area. We probably could have found something in Athens but, having just moved to Rethymnon, we wanted to celebrate here. Eventually we decided to book the White Lady.

Galero Cafe closes at Christmas for the whole of January. Luckily for us we were passing one evening when it was open for a private party. In true Cretan style, we were invited in to join the celebration. We bought our own drinks but had food pressed on us and Robin even got a present from Santa! We never even found out what was being celebrated. That was one of the things Robin loved about living on Crete – the hospitality.

I had decided I did not need to visit the hairdresser before Christmas but booked an appointment between then and New Year; when I thought she would be less busy. Robin had his hair cut first and went down to the Beach Road to wait for me at another cafe we liked called C'est La Vie. Because it was Christmas, we did not stick to our 'no alcohol during the week' rule and he treated himself to a small beer. When I arrived I asked for a Sangria because this was the closest I could get to mulled wine. Before going back to the apartment we shared a club sandwich. They are always served with a mountain of chips here, so are too much for one person.

On New Year's Eve the children are up early again to sing the New Year *Kalanta*. The tradition is also to place a flower bulb, *Scilla Maritima*, outside the threshold to bring good luck for the coming year. People from the village chapels make music in the streets to convey the spirit of Christmas. Families gather at home to feast and celebrate the New Year. The central part of the feast is the *Vasilopita* (Holy Basil Cake) which has a small coin baked into it, much like our Christmas pudding. Cards are then played until dawn while the young people dance the night away in the Bouzouki bars. There is not a large celebration in the town although fireworks are lit at midnight. In the villages you will hear the local farmers discharging their shotguns.

I have to admit I expected the clientele for New Year's Eve to be mostly English people because the venue caters largely for ex-patriots and we thought it would be casual. As a result, we did not dress up. Robin wore a jacket, polo shirt and light trousers. I wore a loose burgundy blouse his sister had bought me for Christmas, with black cropped trousers and my favourite purple suede ankle boots. Most of the other people had dressed for the occasion and we felt a bit under dressed but not completely out of place. There were also a surprising number of Greek people there. We were told later that a lot of local people like to go to the White Lady because it is something different for them.

As mentioned before, Robin had an obsession with getting everywhere early. The New Year's Eve dinner and dancing was scheduled to start at 9 p.m. We took a taxi from the bus station in Rethymnon and arrived at 8.30. We knew there was a set menu but did not realise this included wine and raki. While we were waiting for the rest of the people on our table to arrive, Robin ordered a gin and tonic and I had an ouzo. The owners of the taverna had gone to the trouble of seating us with another English couple who were friendly and outgoing so we felt at ease. This went a long way towards our enjoyment of the evening. We kept in touch afterwards and went out for a couple of meals with them.

The food was also not typically English. We had a meze of starters followed by a Greek mixed grill. By the time we had finished this, we hardly had room for the traditional New Year cake. Every time the wine and raki jugs were emptied, they were replaced. Greek music was played and we were pulled up to dance. At the end of the evening we called a taxi and arrived home at 6 a.m. on New Year's Day – something neither of us had done since we were in our early twenties! It turned out to be a much better evening than either of us anticipated. The only disappointment was that the moment of turning from 2017 to 2018 at midnight was hardly marked, unlike in the UK.

On New Year's Day everyone wants to see who will make the *Podariko* which is the first visitor to set foot in the home, like first footing but without the gifts. Unfortunately the Cretans are a little behind with equal rights and prefer this to be a man. It is said to bring good luck for the whole of the year. Traditionally gifts were distributed by St Basil on 1 January rather than by St Nicholas on Christmas Eve. The tradition of St Basil is still upheld by some Cretan households, whereas some now adhere to Santa Claus. I suspect some lucky Cretan children receive gifts on both days!

As can be imagined, Robin and I did not rise early on New Year's Day. It is a public holiday here, the same as in the UK. I surfaced first. Robin was still fast asleep. With our initial drinks and the flowing wine and raki, we had had a considerable amount to drink the evening before, although it was interspersed with water. The only thing missing was our customary champagne at midnight. Leaving Robin to sleep, I decided to go for a walk. Unlike January in England, I only needed a light jacket. The weather was mild and sunny. People were swimming. I walked round by the Fortezza and decided, despite my homesickness, this was a good place to live.

I thought Robin might be somewhat hung over. Even after 43 years together, he never failed to surprise me. I was deciding what to make myself to eat when he finally surfaced, decided he was hungry, and asked me what I wanted him to cook for dinner. I believe my reply was, 'Anything but turkey!'

We had asked our landlady how to say Happy New Year in Greek and she had told us, *καλή χρονιά* which, literally translated, is good year. She explained that it is also customary to wish people, *χρόνια πολλά* which is many good years. Our downstairs neighbour seemed rather surprised when I wished him a Happy New Year in Greek.

Chapter 12 – Diving for the cross

Since moving to Crete we had heard a lot about diving for the cross. It was talked about in most of the bars and tavernas. As usual, I looked on the internet but could not find very much information. I knew it took place on 6 January and that it concerned the blessing of the waters for the coming year, but there was no information about what time it would take place. I eventually found out that it was 2 p.m., after receiving an email from the White Lady advertising a lunch afterwards.

The Christmas season on Crete does not end with New Year's Day. Epiphany is the climax of the holiday season. It is especially celebrated in style on Crete. It has three names, *Theophania* which means God Shining Forth, *Ta Fota* (or in the singular *Ton Foton*) meaning The Lights (or The Light) and Epiphany. Most people simply refer to it as 'Diving for the Cross.'

For the purpose of this chapter, I will refer to it as *Ta Fota*. It is a celebration of the baptism of Christ in the River Jordan and the revelation of God. Those who have studied the Bible will recall that when Jesus rose up out of the water, the heavens opened and the Holy Spirit came to him as a dove. The voice of God then came to him saying, 'This is my son, the beloved with whom I am well pleased.'

Theophania relates to the Holy Trinity, the voice of the Father coming from heaven, the Son being Jesus and the Holy Spirit coming down from heaven in the form of a dove. *Ta Fota* or

The Lights refers to Christ enlightening the world. As well as celebrating the baptism of Christ, as Christ blessed the waters of the river Jordan, the Orthodox Priests bless all the waters.

The celebration starts on 5 January. Once again, the children come out and sing a special carol announcing the good news of the baptism of Christ. There is a small blessing of the water in church in anticipation of the major event the next day. In the villages, priests go from house to house, blessing the home and family with the holy water and offering the cross to kiss. Many people fast on this day.

So now we come to *Ta Fota* itself. Many people bring bottles and jars to collect the holy water. Some do not drink anything beforehand, so that the first water to pass their lips is the holy water. There is then a procession led by priests and altar boys all in colourful vestments. Church officials also carry banners.

Robin and I arrived at the harbour in good time. I was a little nervous as there were no barriers and I could picture a surge in the crowd pushing me into the water – and I cannot swim! At least Robin was a qualified lifesaver, so I knew he would not let me drown, but I would have preferred not to fall into the cold water. When we arrived, there were not many people around but, as the time moved towards 2 p.m., more and more people were arriving. There were times when Robin's obsession with arriving everywhere early drove me mad, but this was one occasion when it paid off. There were also a number of small boats arriving in the harbour. Tradition has it that no-one sails on the days leading up to *Ta Fota*. The belief is that the blessing will calm the seas so that they will be safer to venture onto.

We had forgotten, of course, that nothing starts on time on Crete, so we had a lengthy wait. The expectation was that all the divers would be hardy men. It came as a surprise then to see, not just adults, but girls and boys who appeared to be as young as eight, waiting in swimsuits with towels round them. In his younger days, Robin had swum in competition. Indeed, his games teacher at school had wanted him to train for the Olympics but, at the time and place where he grew up, his priority was to leave school and start earning a living. I suggested he might like to have a go at diving for the cross himself. Although the weather was mild and sunny, he declined, saying, 'I bet that water is bloody cold!'

Eventually the procession arrived. By this time, there were so many people along the harbour-side and boats in the water; we could only just see what was going on. There was a lengthy blessing which, of course, we could not understand because it was in Greek. Excitement was mounting and the crowd was pressing closer to the harbour. I held onto Robin tightly. Then came the dramatic moment, in went the cross, followed in quick succession by the divers. At the same time, all the boats sounded their horns and set off flares. We noted that there was a rope attached to the cross in the event that none of the divers were able to retrieve it. I am happy to say on this occasion that was not the case. The person who retrieves the cross receives a special blessing. At the same time, the priest releases a dove that symbolises the Holy Spirit.

We missed the procession to the harbour but were able to quickly slip through an alleyway and view it on its return to the church. In addition to the procession, there was also a band playing. For a large number of years we had been involved with the Scouts and all our children played in a Scout and Guide band at one time or another. As a result, Robin always had an interest in marching bands, so we stayed to watch until they were out of sight and earshot.

On returning to the church, there is a vat of holy water and a branch of basil by the altar. This is the time when people fill the containers they have brought. The basil is dipped in the holy water and the priest uses it to make the sign of the cross on the foreheads and shoulders of each member of the congregation. Everyone in the household will drink the holy water, including the animals. It is even sprinkled over the plants!

Of course not being Greek Orthodox, Robin and I did not follow the procession back to the church. We decided to try to find somewhere to have a snack for lunch. This proved far more difficult than anticipated! Cretan people are very family orientated. Most Sundays you will find families gathering together in the tavernas for an extended lunch. Many village tavernas will spit roast lamb and serve it with fried potatoes on Sunday afternoons.

As this was such a special occasion, even more families were out and about. All the tavernas along the seafront were full. We eventually managed to find a couple of high stools at a table in Chaplin's. Chaplin's is a rock pub and not somewhere you would want to go in the evening if you value your eardrums. Nevertheless, it is slightly quieter during the day and we found it a pleasant place to drink a beer (Robin), glass of wine (me) and share a club sandwich. We went there quite a lot at weekends in the New Year and they got to know us. After lunch I would often be given a shot of ouzo and Robin would be treated to a shot of five-star Metaxa. He was not really a brandy drinker back in the UK but he acquired quite a taste for five-star Metaxa.

It was difficult not to get caught up in the general holiday atmosphere. People were making the most of the end of the Christmas season before the general dreariness of January set in. Of course, the view out across the flawless blue sea with the Venetian Harbour to our left and the Marina to our right, all added to the occasion. We were still new enough residents to have our hearts stirred by the scene.

Epiphany also marks the end of the *Kalikantzari's* mischief. Legend has it that these small goblins arrive at Christmas to cause mayhem. The light of God and the blessing of the waters are said to drive them underground until the following Christmas. They are thought to be mainly a domestic nuisance but some people also blame them for the rough seas. I am happy to say that they did not wreak any havoc in our apartment!

Chapter 13 – Getting our health books and other frustrations

The next few chapters are written in sequence but they overlap and cover different events that occurred within the same period of time.

Our first few weeks in our new home were taken up with finding our way round and preparing for Christmas. Now the honeymoon period was over and we had to start thinking about important matters such as sorting out health care and making a tax declaration.

The first CIC coffee morning of 2018 took place on the Monday after Epiphany. Attending was useful because we were told what we needed in the way of documentation to apply for our health books. This time we walked there through the town. We made our way back along the Beach Road and Robin was enthralled to see the White Mountains in the distance covered in snow. On sea level the sun was shining and there were even one or two people on sun beds on the beach.

On Crete, people do not register with a GP, as they do in the UK. They are issued with a health book by IKA, which is the equivalent of the NHS. If a visit to the doctor is needed, one goes to the hospital or other designated IKA heath centre. The health book is then produced and the appropriate notes made in it. Greece and the UK have a reciprocal arrangement whereby UK citizens who are in receipt of the UK pension (I

hate to use the term 'pensioner' in relation to myself) are entitled to the same free healthcare as Greek citizens. Recompense
is then sought by IKA from the NHS.

You may think this would be easy but you would be wrong!
The process did not turn out to be anywhere near as simple as
we thought. The UK government issues each person with two
S1 forms. Unlike everything else we did, they could not be
issued until we were resident in Greece. The first lot of forms
went astray, so a further set had to be sent. These had to be
completed by IKA who would then keep one copy and send
the other back to the UK.

We went to the IKA office with our forms, residents' permits
and passports. The first thing we were asked for was an AMKA
number. This turned out to be the Greek equivalent of a
National Insurance number. We did not have these and were
directed to the KEP office to obtain them. The KEP office was
duly attended with all the documents we thought might be
required. We were told we could not be issued with AMKA
numbers because we were not working on Crete. The IKA office
is a couple of kilometres uphill above the town so we decided
not to make the trek back that day. Instead, we returned the
following week. On trying to explain that the KEP office would
not give us AMKA numbers, the staff at the IKA office insisted
they could not issue us with health books without AMKA
numbers. So, we paid another visit to the KEP office to explain
the position but we were still refused AMKA numbers.

At this point I realised there was no point going backwards
and forwards. IKA would not give us health books without
AMKA numbers and KEP would not issue us with AMKA
numbers because we were not working on Crete. We were

just going round in circles. I contacted the British Consulate in Heraklion and explained the position. They contacted the KEP office who eventually agreed to provide us with AMKA numbers. The lady at the British Consulate was very helpful and said we should contact her from the KEP office if we had any further problems.

The only further problem we had was that, although we had all the documents we thought we could possibly need, we did not have our birth certificates! Fortunately our apartment was close enough to town for us to walk back and collect them. At last, we were issued with our AMKA numbers. The man at the KEP office did apologise and said they had to be careful that we were not illegal immigrants. The fact that Robin, in particular, did not look old enough to be retired probably had not helped. I had always joked with him that the reason he never seemed to age was the portrait he kept in the attic, like Dorian Grey!

On returning to the IKA office we were given forms to complete. They were all in Greek and we were not offered any assistance. Having worked for a local authority, I can understand this. We were often asked by people to help fill in their claim forms. We were not allowed to do that because we could be accused of not being impartial when deciding the claim. Luckily for Robin and me, a man waiting at the next counter spoke good English and helped us.

Again, we thought we had everything we needed only to find that we needed two copies of our passports and we only had one of each! Robin went downstairs to find somewhere to copy them while I kept our place in the queue. The people at the downstairs office told him they could not do the copying. He went outside to a kiosk to ask where he could make some copies. To his surprise the man in the kiosk said he could do them there. I suspect this was a regular occurrence. After being sent to a couple of different offices in the building, we were finally given our books there and then. On walking back to town I remember saying to Robin, 'I think you deserve a pint!'

Strangely enough, he did not argue with me...

It was about this time that we realised we had to renew our passports. Back in early 2018 it was still possible to complete the renewal form online; print it and send it, with the required documents, to the Passport Office. The problem was that we were asked to return our old passports. Although we had our residents' permits, everything we needed to do seemed to depend upon showing our passports. I took photocopies of our passports and sent these, along with a covering letter explaining the position. Following a lengthy telephone conversation with the Passport Office, it became clear that there was no way they were going to issue us with new passports unless we sent off our old ones.

The irony is that, once our new passports had been sent, the old ones were returned to us! Of course, on going to the post office to collect our new passports we were asked, 'Passports please.'

Fortunately, the post office staff all speak good English and when I explained the position, they accepted our residents' permits and driving licences.

We found out quite by accident that we would need to file a tax declaration, even though we were paying tax in the UK. I was somewhat worried about this because we did not want to pay tax in two countries. Also, the rate is higher in Greece than in the UK and the Greek tax system gives a smaller personal allowance.

At this time we were living on our pensions only so every penny counted. We were recommended to an accountant who spoke English and made an appointment. Along we went with every conceivable document I thought we could possibly need. I printed off statements from all our bank accounts, together with our pensions. The first thing she said to us was,

'You live here all year round but pay tax in the UK?'

'Yes,' we replied.

She asked us this several times but I had already checked with our UK accountant and he did not see a problem with it, especially as we still owned a property in the UK.

It turned out that all she needed by way of documentation was a form from the bank; showing the money we had transferred from our UK account to open a Greek bank account. This, of course was the one thing we did not have!

This meant another lengthy queue in the bank. Because Greece has not yet entered the internet age, most people go to the bank or the post office to pay their bills. This is why there is always such a queue. Robin had far more patience than me and just accepted it philosophically, whereas I became frustrated. Eventually, we were supplied with the document we needed and took it back to the accountant.

We also found that, once we had opened an account, staff at the bank were less than helpful. The account was originally opened using our UK address. When changing our address with our UK banks, we simply went online and changed it. Although we had online banking for our Greek bank account, this facility was not available. We decided to do this at the same time as getting the document for the accountant, to save another visit. Our request was flatly refused without us producing a utility bill showing our address on Crete. Of course, we could not do this because our apartment was rented and the bills were not in our name. Even after explaining that we no longer lived at the UK address, we could not change it. I later found out that our Greek address could be added as a secondary address and I was able to have a debit card sent to it. This made absolutely no sense.

On returning to the accountant she asked, 'Would you like me to deal with the tax office on your behalf?'

'Yes please,' we said.

The idea of having to deal with the staff in the tax office did not appeal, following on from our experience with obtaining our tax numbers. We would never have done it without help from the lawyer. To enable the accountant to represent us, we needed to complete powers of attorney. Naturally, these had to be taken to the KEP office to be witnessed.

The final thing was that, after over forty years together, our marriage had to be registered at the Town Hall. To do this we had to lodge a formalised copy of our marriage certificate. I did not want to risk losing the original, so I ordered a copy from the Register of Births, Marriages and Deaths. This then had to be sent to the Foreign Office for formalisation. Once that was received, we were finally all set. The accountant said, 'Now we can get you married.'

When we told our landlady she said we should have a party to celebrate our 'marriage'!

It was part of our plan to learn to speak Greek. Our view was that if we were going to live in a foreign country, we should at least make an effort to learn some of the language. I was going to go to lessons but Robin said he would learn better by hearing people speak. He did seem to have the knack of picking things up quickly. I was learning the Greek alphabet and I remember him saying to me quite soon after we moved, 'That letter that looks like a circle with a line through it is an 'f' isn't it?'

Despite this, he had difficultly pronouncing the name of the road we lived in, so he cut the address part from one of our change of address cards and kept it in his wallet. He also had the good idea of writing our tax and AMKA numbers on cards. He kept one in his wallet and I kept one in my purse. We soon found out that almost everything depended on us being able to quote our tax numbers.

Things were not all bad though. Despite the pitfalls of Greek bureaucracy, there are a lot of benefits to living on Crete. One of these is that Cretans believe in repairing things. In the UK whenever you take something to be repaired, you usually get a sharp intake of breath followed by the statement, 'It'll be much cheaper to throw it away and buy new.'

Robin had a pair of casual leather shoes he bought on our first visit to Rethymnon. He loved them because they were so comfortable. Although the uppers were leather, the soles were moulded rubber and they were worn out. There was no way a cobbler in the UK would mend them. Robin took them to the shoe repairer here who was quite happy to sole and heel them. Robin was so happy to get them repaired; I have kept them in his memory box.

A number of people had said to us that they would not like to live on a Greek island because they are filthy. While on our numerous visits here, Robin had disagreed with this view, commenting that wherever we went there were always people cleaning. This is perfectly true. I think the problem is that, while people keep their homes spotlessly clean, they do have a habit of dumping rubbish in the street or out in the countryside. This is difficult to understand in a country where the refuse collectors will take away anything left by the bins, even garden rubbish, unlike in the UK where a collection of garden waste or builders' rubble has to be paid for.

Here on Crete households do not have their own rubbish and recycling containers. Large bins for rubbish and mixed recycling are placed at strategic points around the neighbourhood. As a result, refuse collection takes place every day, even Christmas Day and Easter Sunday. The dustcart comes round very early in the morning and I must admit, at first, it woke us up every morning. After a couple of weeks, however, we got used to it and slept through. Although I missed my job, it was something of a relief to no longer have to get up a 5.30 a.m. for the commute to London.

There were a worrying few days when the refuse collectors went on strike. As you can imagine, it piled up very quickly and, in this warm climate, could very soon become a health hazard. As it turned out, the dispute was resolved within a short space of time and the rubbish cleared speedily.

As previously stated, our original intention had been to sell our house in the UK. This would provide us with enough money to buy two reasonable sized villas here and one small one. The idea would then be to live in one and rent out the other two. I was concerned about the length of time our house had stood empty and there had been little interest from prospective buyers. This was, no doubt, due to the Christmas and New Year period but the agent we had placed it with did not seem to be making very much effort.

Renting it out seemed a much better option and we worked out that this would produce a higher rental income in the UK than we could expect on Crete, even for two properties. The other deciding factor was that there are only villas in villages and we did not want to live in a village. All we could buy in the town would be an apartment with the attendant problems of the Greek equivalent of ground rent and service charges. Of course, having made the move only a few weeks ago, we were also settled in our apartment and were not anxious to move once again. We had lived in our UK house for over thirty years, most of which had been happy, so I was pleased we were not selling it. I can recall Robin collecting me from the station after work one evening and calling it 'our little castle' when pulling onto the driveway.

Robin contacted a former colleague who was a builder. He agreed to undertake the necessary work and obtain all the requisite certificates, such as gas safe. The work took longer than anticipated because it coincided with the 'beast from the east' that hit the UK in early 2018. At the same time we were going out during the daytime in light jackets and sunglasses! It was even warm enough to sit outside at lunchtime with our coffee during the week or beer and glass of wine at the weekend.

Once the work was completed we put the house back on the market for rent. The first agent (who was recommended to us) was disparaging about the house saying that the kitchen and bathroom were outdated and needed replacing. Concern was also expressed about the size of Robin's workshop at the end of the garden. The general theme was that we needed to attract people with young families and our house would not do that; everything needed to be modernised. This reduced me to tears because I loved that little house and thought we would end up having to sell it after all. It also hurt to think that the kitchen Robin fitted with such care might have to be ripped out and replaced.

As usual, Robin was the voice of reason. He comforted me and said he would speak to his builder friend, who said the agent was talking nonsense. The house was in good condition and the amount of extra income we would get by replacing the kitchen and bathroom was not worth the outlay. We therefore approached the agent who valued the property back in the summer. He was happy to place it on the market for rent as it stood. It took very little time for interest to be shown and Robin's workshop was a help rather than a hindrance. One of the original tenants was a builder and could make use of it. Unfortunately, Robin died before the rental contract was signed but at least he knew it was going through.

The January lunch for the CIC was in town which made a pleasant change for us because we could walk there. It took place at Othonas, where we were regulars, it being one of the few restaurants to open during the winter. Even though it was January, we sat at the area in front with the roof open and were not cold. Nick and Adrienne were not able to attend this time but by now we had got to know many of the other members. I sat next to some French people and was pleased to find I could manage to carry out a basic conversation with them in my schoolgirl French. I also recall Robin speaking to a German man about his joinery and how he was hoping to do some part time work here, once he had a workshop set up.

Before we left the UK, Robin was due for a check-up with the dentist. By this time, he was well overdue for a clean and polish and was starting to get toothache. I looked up English speaking dentists on the 'Living in Crete' website and found several in Rethymnon. We located one in an easily accessible area and I made Robin an appointment. The session went well and he was charged far less than he would have been by a private dentist in the UK. More importantly, Robin liked the dentist. I remember he made an appointment for me and one for his next 6 monthly check-up. On leaving, the dentist said, 'Have a good summer and I'll see you in August.'

Strangely enough, when we mentioned him to Adrienne and Nick, they said he was also their dentist and they were very pleased with him.

We were starting to fit in with the Cretan lifestyle and Robin, in particular, was thoroughly enjoying it. I remember him coming home one day and saying, 'I am awash with coffee!' He had met the waiter from the Globe who had insisted on buying him a coffee. They sat and had a chat. Then on the way back to the apartment he passed the back entrance to the Globe. We had not realised this was part of the Globe although we knew it was open for takeaway in the winter. The owner was making crepes for takeaway. He had also insisted on buying Robin a coffee and having a chat. That was what Robin loved about being here. People recognised him and were friendly.

Chapter 14 – Setting up work

We had always believed the Cretans were very hard working. It therefore came as something of a surprise to find out that many people retire at age sixty. This is, of course, probably as a result of the long hours they work. Shops open early in the morning and many stay open as late as 11 p.m. The same staff seem to be on duty for the whole of the opening hours. After closing, they are still there clearing up ready for the next day.

The same goes for bars and restaurants. Often the staff do not even have a day off during the week in the summer season. Of course, many of the establishments are closed during the winter so the staff are not employed then. However, some do take on other work during the winter break. Businesses catering for the tourist trade have to rely on making enough money during the summer to cover the lack of income in the winter.

Now Christmas was past, we really needed to decide what to do with our time. In the lead up to Christmas we were settling in and planning for Christmas, so time seemed to go quickly. Before leaving the UK we were both working. I was full-time but Robin had cut down his hours over the previous couple of years, although he still enjoyed what he did. I was not really ready to give up my job but I knew we had to make the move then or we would never do it. Unfortunately, I was homesick at times and now deeply regret letting Robin see it.

Both of us only wanted to work part-time. A large part of our desire to move to Crete was to be able to spend more time together, but we also wanted time to pursue our hobbies. At one time I was a keen amateur dressmaker. I made my own wedding and bridesmaids' dresses and a lot of the children's clothes. My skills were stretched to the limit when I was called upon to make five blue velvet bridesmaids' dresses for my brother's first marriage. As time went by and my job became more demanding, I had very little time for this.

Part of the furniture that came with the apartment was a large computer desk. This was in the front bedroom when we moved in. There was also a smaller desk, with drawers, in the living room, which was much more suitable for my laptop and printer. Robin set this up for me as part of a work-station in an area with the most natural light. He also moved the large desk into the small bedroom. It was ideal for laying out fabric to cut out. I was also able to leave my sewing out instead of having to clear everything away when I had finished for the day. I also kept my knitting and spare yarn in there, so it became known as 'the craft room.'

As I mentioned previously, Robin was able to return to his hobby of sketching and also to spend more time pottering around in the kitchen. He would happily spend most of the morning poring over recipe books to decide what to cook. He would then spend the afternoons, when I was working, preparing and cooking our evening meal. When I was working or sewing he would often pop his head round the corner and say, 'Fancy a coffee?'

There were a number of options I considered for paid work. I had always wanted to write a novel and had started on this before Christmas but had only written the opening chapters. Proofreading was also another option for working remotely.

I consulted a number of recruitment websites and even the National Careers Advisory Service but received very little positive feedback. I found things are very different now from when I had been job seeking before. Online recruitment agencies expected me to know what I wanted to do and I had to put a specific job title into the search function. Even then it was difficult to link some of the options that came up to the job title entered! There seemed to be little advice online for people like me who just needed to know what was available to them.

Robin thought I would make a good tour guide, despite the fact that I cannot speak Greek! I did approach Thompson. I completed their online application form and was offered an interview, for which I would have to travel to London. That was not a problem because, by this time, we were considering making a visit back to the UK. Although I had explained that I had recently moved to Crete and was looking for work here, one of the specifications was that I had to be prepared to work anywhere. Having just moved to Crete, I had no desire to be offered a position that meant spending the summer in Spain or Italy, for example.

Again, Robin came up trumps. In my UK job I worked for two local authorities. The first handled the claims for the second under contract. I was therefore based in the office of one and worked for the other one remotely. Robin thought there was a good chance I might still be able to work for one of them remotely from Crete. When I left, my employer told me if it did not work out on Crete and I returned to the UK wanting my old job back, the authority would do its best to accommodate me. I had kept in touch and sent out a few hints. Robin told me to ask outright. I had nothing to lose and he said, 'If you don't ask, you don't get.'

I contacted my old boss and offered to work remotely for three days a week. That would be enough to give me an interest outside the home and still leave time to spend with Robin. My boss was very keen on the idea but said he would have to get the OK from his immediate superior. In a very short time the answer came back in the affirmative. I was to be on a temporary contract, renewable every six months, beginning at the end of January. I recall he sent me an email saying, 'There's no backing out now!'

I had no intention of doing that.

Next came the setting up of remote working. Because I had previously worked remotely for one local authority under contract to the other, it had always been done in the office. Now I had to set up the correct software. This was a bit of a nightmare. While I can search the internet, send emails, use the word processing facility and a case management system, when it came to setting up software, I was completely lost. Robin was no help. He was a complete technophobe, his answer being, 'You can't do my job on a computer.'

Before we moved he said learning to use the laptop was on his bucket list but his enthusiasm had waned by the time we arrived. Nevertheless, I managed to sort it all out with help from the IT department.

Of course, my boss was not able to visit to ensure all the correct procedures were being complied with, so I needed to complete forms to show that all the health and safety requirements for home working were in place. I also had to buy a proper adjustable office chair. Until now I had been using one of the dining chairs, which was far from ideal. Fortunately there was a shop that sold second-hand furniture close to our apartment. They had a couple of office chairs for a reasonable price. I remember Robin carrying it home and saying, 'Tell your boss he owes me a drink for carrying this chair home!'

I did suggest he could wheel it home but he said that would ruin the wheels. I recall sending a photo to my boss, noting that it was luminous green but it least it did not clash with our dark green carpet.

I worked on UK time so I started at 11 a.m. Greek time and finished at 7 p.m. Robin often joked with me when we got up in the morning saying, 'Hurry up or you'll be late for work!'

and I would reply, 'Yes, all this travelling is really tiring!'

At least I no longer had to get up at 5.30 a.m. so it did not matter if we had a late night the day before.

We did not have fitted carpets, just a couple of rugs on top of the tiled floor. This made cleaning fairly easy. I would go round with the broom and Robin would follow with the mop and bucket. He would occasionally brush the large rug in the living area in between times, saying, 'Don't mind me, I'm just Hoovering the carpet!'

When I was working Robin would often go for a walk in the morning and spent a lot of time talking to our landlady in her shop. She told me afterwards that he had said to her, 'Marilyn must be good at her job if they're letting her work from here.'

He was always proud of me.

Robin still wanted to do some woodwork as it was his passion as well as his trade. Before doing this he had two problems to overcome. The first was finding somewhere he could set up as a workshop and the second was having transport to collect timber and other materials. There was what looked like a disused garage under our apartment building. He asked our landlady if he could use it but, although it was not being used, it belonged to the furniture shop on the ground floor. Our landlady did, however, say there was a large basement under the building, used mostly for storage, and Robin was welcome to use part of it as a workshop. He came back to the apartment with the keys in his hand and a huge grin on his face.

One of the flats below us is occupied by a wood carver who owns several shops in the town. Although he spoke very little English and Robin spoke no Greek, they managed to communicate with one another. He said he had a bench saw he did not use and, if Robin was interested, he would sell it to him. This was a good start because Robin had sold all his large machinery before leaving the UK. He had only brought hand tools and small electrical equipment with him. Our neighbour also said if Robin wanted to make small items suitable for tourists, such as trinket boxes, he would sell them in his shop for him.

Shortly before we returned to the UK for Easter, Robin went out for a walk and popped into our landlady's shop for a chat. Her sister was there and asked Robin if he could put up some shelves in her kitchen. He was happy to agree – he had his first commission!

Robin really liked his Greek yoghurt. He also used it in a lot of recipes as a healthy alternative to cream. We used to buy it in large pots. Over the next few weeks Robin started washing out the yoghurt pots to use for storing his nails and screws. All we needed now was a set of wheels. During the week before we left for the UK, our neighbour said he would be happy to drive Robin to the builders' merchants to buy what he needed. I had also ordered from Amazon some music box movements, small hinges and green and red baize to line the trinket boxes.

I am happy to say that I still have some items that Robin made. One is a large jewellery box he made for my late mother. When we moved I took out the inserts and used it to store our important documents. I also have a small jewellery box he made for one of our daughters, where I keep my USB drives. Finally, there is the wooden carrying case he made for my sewing machine.

The February lunch for the CIC was at Sfakaki, where we nearly bought a villa. We both agreed that it was our good fortune that we were not able to take out an equity release to do so. It is much too far away from town and we would have been isolated there. Adrienne and Nick were able to attend this one. Robin's sister had bought him two sets of cuff links for Christmas. One set was a hammer and saw and the other was spirit levels. On this day, Robin wore the spirit levels and I recall him joking with Nick and saying, 'It's OK if I get drunk, these'll tell me if I'm upright!'

We still liked to go out to eat at weekends. I recall one Saturday at about this time when we had quite a large lunch so we were not hungry in the evening. Instead of going out for a meal, we went to Galero and had a couple of drinks. At about 10 p.m. Robin decided he was hungry and wanted pitta gyros. We walked from one end of the town to the other to find somewhere where we could get just a pitta gyros but not a full meal. There were plenty of takeaways but we wanted to be able to sit down. Eventually we found somewhere and Robin got his pitta gyros. I would not have minded but I had dressed up for the evening and was wearing heels. By the time we got home I could hardly walk!

Chapter 15 – Carnival

Even out of the tourist season, there always seems to be something happening on Crete. Now Epiphany was over, the bars and tavernas started advertising *Καρναβάλι* (Carnival). Most of the outlying villages also have their own team. As soon as the Christmas decorations were taken down, mannequins arrived wearing the costumes for that year's carnival team. It was not necessary to be invited to join a team; we just had to decide which costume we liked and ask if we could join. Robin was a great Sherlock Holmes fan so the deerstalkers and checked capes appealed to him. I rather liked the pack of cards that was the theme of Galero's team. Chaplin's costumes were of 1920s flappers, which I also liked. Of course, it was a bit soon for us to join a team; we were just looking forward to watching the procession. We did not realise at the time that it was not just a one day event.

As well as costumes appearing in all the bars and tavernas, posters were put up in shops advertising the various teams. Papier mache statutes from previous years' floats were placed at strategic points all over town. I recall one morning Robin came in from the balcony and informed me there was a giraffe across the road. I thought he was hallucinating but, sure enough, on a small grassy area on the corner, there was a statue of a giraffe!

If you live in Rethymnon, it is almost impossible not to get caught up in the excitement of the lead up to the Carnival. We loved seeing all the different costumes in the shops and the statues from previous floats all over town. I can recall one of a bull dressed up as a boxer on the Beach Road and a lady in burlesque costume, playing a violin, on the roundabout heading into Kalithea. There was even one outside the IKA office when we went to get our health books.

Rethymnon Carnival attracts over 40,000 visitors a year and is the third largest in Greece. The tradition has been ongoing since 1914. The date depends on when Easter falls, because this is the last celebration before the fasting and self-denial of Lent. It is certainly a bit different from Pancake Day! Thousands of volunteers give up their time to organise this event which, of course, brings much needed business into the town. As I discovered later when I joined a team for the Carnival, planning starts as early as November and the teams meet on a regular basis from then onwards. Each team has its own social events leading up to the Carnival itself.

The official celebrations begin about a month before the big parade, when the Carnival King walks through the town. On his arrival at *Platia Agnostou Stratioti* (the square of the Unknown Soldier), known locally as Soldier Square, the Mayor officially opens the Carnival and presents the theme and crews. This is followed by music and dance.

Over the coming weeks there are various events including treasure hunts and musical evenings. The Thursday before the parade is *Tsiknopempti*, or Grill Thursday, It is also sometimes known as Smelly Thursday. I am not sure why it is called that. I can only assume it is from the smell of the barbecues. This was Robin's and my first involvement in the celebrations. Our landlady's partner was in Thessaloniki visiting family but she invited us to join her with family and friends. We met at her shop, with her sister and two nephews, and walked down to the Beach Road.

Everywhere there were barbecues set up. As we walked into town from our apartment, we noticed even the staff at the local supermarket were outside with a small barbecue. The town was packed and we were offered free wine and food. After meeting some Belgian friends of our landlady, who now live here, we went to a nearby taverna for food and wine. Then we spent the rest of the evening listening to live music. Robin particularly enjoyed the rock 'n' roll. It was a great evening and, in spite of the high spirits, everyone was good natured and there was no trouble.

It is usually about this time that scaffolding towers are put up along the route to hold the sound systems. We walked into town at some point almost every day, so we watched with growing enthusiasm as everything started to take shape and the Carnival atmosphere grew.

On the Saturday afternoon before the Grand Parade, there is a children's parade and in the evening a parade of last year's costumes. Our plan had been to watch the parade of last year's costumes but things did not always work out the way we planned. We had a snack lunch at Galero that day. The smell of waffles was tantalising our taste buds but Robin wanted ice cream. We should have stayed at Galero as they do a good range of ice cream. There are a number of ice cream shops in the Old Town but Robin wanted to sit down to eat it, so we ended up at a place on the Beach Road. We ordered a combination for two but instead of just ice cream, we ended up with waffles and chocolate sauce as well. By the time we were finished, we were completely full and feeling slightly sick.

Robin nicknamed the place 'Chocolate Sick' for reasons that will later become apparent.

We were told that the evening parade would be in the square. Unfortunately, we went to Soldier Square. Instead it finished at the square outside Four Martyrs Church, unsurprisingly known locally as Four Martyrs Square! At least missing the parade guaranteed us a seat at Galero and we were still able to see many people in their previous year's costumes.

After our ice cream and chocolate fest earlier in the day, we were not hungry so we had a couple of glasses of wine. It was a fantastic evening. Most of the Galero team were in their costumes from the previous year and the staff were all dressed up. People were really enjoying themselves. Music was playing. Everyone was dancing and really letting their hair down. That was the last time Robin and I jived together. He was so happy and having a good time.

By about midnight we were beginning to feel hungry, not to mention slightly light headed from drinking wine without eating. We knew a place called Kokkinos that is open 24 hours a day where we could get pitta gyros so we headed there. There is no MacDonald's in Rethymnon, so this is the Cretan equivalent. It sells burgers but the pitta gyros is the most popular item on the menu. It also serves alcohol. One thing we noticed early in our travels to the Greek Islands is that alcohol is served almost everywhere, even in the cafes at museums and places of interest.

En route to Kokkinos we passed Othonas where the waiter (who knew us) asked if we were hungry. Although this was after midnight, we were invited in for a meal. The other people in the taverna dragged us up to do the conga. All told, it was a lovely evening and we arrived home in the early hours tired, but happy.

Unfortunately, Robin spent a lot of the rest of the night in the bathroom. We put this down to the waffles and chocolate we had eaten the day before. Neither of us realised at the time that it was probably a symptom of his illness. Nevertheless, he was up and on the balcony reasonably early the following day. The yard belonging to the Municipality of Rethymnon, where many of the floats were being stored, was close to our apartment, so they were driven past on their way to the starting point. Robin excitedly called me out onto the balcony saying, 'Look, they are taking the floats down!'

The parade was due to start at 2 p.m. but we decided to walk down early to make sure we were able to get a good position. We were so early we had time to grab a coffee in Four Martyrs Square, where we thought would be the best place to watch from. We were able to get a place at the front. Unlike most things on Crete, Carnival actually starts on time. We waited with excitement for the first float to arrive. That year the sponsor was Amstel and the first arrivals were roller skaters, dressed as Smurfs, carrying letters spelling out Amstel in Greek. Some of the roller skaters were quite small children; we were really impressed with their skill.

Teams include people of all ages, from young children, up to people in their 60s and 70s, or older if they are fit enough to walk the route. Quite a number of the younger men actually dress up in the women's costumes. Robin would have definitely stuck to the men's costume, although I have seen him dress as a woman when we were Scout leaders and used to take part in Gang Shows.

One particular occasion that comes to mind was when he dressed in a tutu for a rendition of the Dance of the Cygnets. He was always game for a laugh. Several of the young men would climb up onto the scaffolding towers that held the sound equipment, and dance there. I could see Robin doing that because he spent a large part of his working life climbing around on scaffolding!

People in costume walk alongside the floats rather than ride on them. Everyone is dancing and blowing whistles or horns. Streamers and confetti were thrown. I remember thinking I would not want to be a road sweeper the following day. I suspect quite a lot of raki is also consumed along the way.

Robin suffered from claustrophobia and, after a while, he found the press of people behind us oppressive. I was a bit worried about where he had gone, especially as he had been unwell during the night. There were plenty of Red Cross personnel in attendance but I did not want him to pass out and end up in hospital, even though we now had our health books. As it turned out, he went up the steps outside Four

Martyrs Church and was able to see everything from there. I was glad he had not missed out.

When the crowd thinned out a bit, he was able to come back to join me – just in time to see a man from one of the teams grab my hand and twirl me round. He always loved to see me enjoying myself. If I have one criticism of the Carnival it is that there is often quite a delay between floats. This interrupts the continuity and can make parts of the parade boring.

Robin was still feeling slightly unwell so we went home after the parade. As a result we missed the concluding ceremony on the Beach Road and the burning of the Carnival King's chariot.

The following day is known as Clean Monday or Ash Monday, which sees the end of the celebration period. It is the last day of feasting before the 40 days of Lent and also includes events such as kite flying. There are various activities going on in the outlying villages.

Once this is over, everything falls a bit flat for a few weeks. Many of the bars and tavernas that were open just for the Carnival close again until the start of the summer season, usually early April or Easter time. As you may have already guessed, Cretans on the whole are devout Orthodox Christians and take the Lent fasting seriously. I recall passing one of our favourite restaurants, *Prassein Aloga* (Greek for the Green Horse). We told the waiter we would see him on Saturday evening for a meal and he asked us if we would be eating meat or sticking to fish as it was Lent.

Easter is the main celebration in the Orthodox calendar, much more important than Christmas. The Orthodox Easter is often a week or so later than the Anglican or Catholic Easter, so we would be able to celebrate it with our family in the UK and also on Crete. Our landlady had invited us to celebrate it with her family and we were very much looking forward to it.

Chapter 16 – Looking for a car

Before leaving the UK we sold our car and Robin's van. We then put the money into a separate account to fund the purchase of a car when we had settled in Rethymnon. We were somewhat disappointed at how much we were offered for the car by various garages we approached and 'We Buy Any Car' on the internet. It was only three years old, in good condition, with low mileage. In the end, a work colleague of Robin's bought both the car and the van from us for a very good price.

That said, and bearing in mind that the cost of living is much lower for most things on Crete, we expected to be able to buy a good second hand car with the money we had available. Unfortunately, we were wrong. Cretans tend to buy new and run the car for about 20 years until it falls apart. It is usually then pushed over a cliff or used as a dog kennel or outbuilding for livestock.

Once I had established my remote working pattern and we had some income in addition to our pensions, we decided it was time to start looking for a car. We had managed quite well so far without. Our apartment was within easy walking distance of the town. With one or two exceptions, vehicles are banned from the Old Town during the daytime and evenings in the summer season. The streets are very narrow and parking is difficult. Anyone who wants to use a vehicle usually has a motorcycle or scooter.

Now, motorcycles are one of the downsides to living on

Crete. A Greek acquaintance once said that they are like cockroaches and I would not disagree. They do not consider themselves 'vehicles' and drive around the Old Town at all times of day, far too fast. One has to be extremely careful on pedestrian crossings. Robin nearly got hit by a motorcycle overtaking a car that had stopped for him at a crossing. He also had a narrow miss from one being ridden the wrong way along a one way street. If they want to go somewhere, they do not think twice about riding along the footpath or cycle track.

Another regular occurrence is parking on the footpath, thus forcing pedestrians to walk on the cycle track. In addition, youngsters riding mopeds seem to think if they tune them up to make as much noise as possible, people will think they are proper motorcycles. At night they treat the main road as a race track and always seem to rev up right outside our apartment. Keep your wits about you when driving because they overtake on both sides!

A bout of meningitis several years ago left Robin prone to motion sickness. He also felt uncomfortable not being in control, which is probably why he was such a 'back seat driver' when I was behind the wheel, despite telling everyone I was a good driver. He hated public transport and suffered flying only because it was taking him to the exotic destinations he wanted to visit. The local bus service is very good, cheap and reliable, but we needed a car so that we could get out and about at weekends.

Crete is the largest of the Greek Islands. Although we had visited many times, there were a number of places too far away from where we were staying to be able to visit in a day. Our aim was to explore these parts of the island by staying for two or three days at a time. To do this, we needed a car. Robin also needed the car to pick up tools and woodworking materials. The other thing a car would be useful for was driving to the airport for visits to the UK and to collect visitors.

Our search for a suitable car was hampered by the fact that Cretans do very little online. The waiter at Galero was helpful. He looked cars for sale up on his phone but we needed to call the people selling them and, of course, we could only speak a few words of Greek. Robin was not keen on buying privately, preferring to go to a garage and have some sort of guarantee.

Although it was much easier to walk into town from our apartment, we were beginning to feel a little frustrated at not having our own transport. Neither of us had been without a car since we passed our driving tests. I did manage to find a couple of what looked like car showrooms online and made a note of the addresses.

When we were looking for the KEP and IKA offices, we bought a street map of Rethymnon. One of the car showrooms appeared to be within walking distance, so we set off armed with our street map. The problem turned out to be that not all streets have names on them. They are named on the map but not in the flesh so to speak. After a number of wrong turns and walking what seemed like miles, we finally found out that it was a garage that carried out servicing but did not sell cars. This was another occasion when Robin enjoyed a well-earned pint at Chaplin's!

We then decided we needed to hire a car to look for a car. I mentioned before that there is a good bus service here but it would not allow us the flexibility to visit car showrooms. Of course, in February there are not many car hire businesses open and I was surprised at how much they were charging for even a basic model. I made what I thought was an enquiry online and then decided not to proceed. This was on a Thursday. I was only working Monday to Wednesday so we were looking to hire a car for the next day, being Friday.

The next thing I knew, on Friday morning Robin and I were shopping in the local supermarket when his mobile rang. I had given the car hire company Robin's number because he had a Greek phone whereas I had retained my UK one. The person asked for me and Robin handed the phone over. I was asked when I would be collecting the car I had hired for that day! I apologised, explained that I thought I had only made an enquiry and asked if we could have the car the following day, Saturday, instead.

We duly collected the car the next day and explained that we were looking to buy a car. The man at the car hire company said they would be looking to sell some of their current range at the beginning of the season; he would look out for something suitable for us.

Off we went to look at a car we had seen advertised online. It was an elderly Suzuki Jimny that appeared to have a low mileage. We had been thinking about a four wheel drive that would not struggle on some of the mountain roads. On arrival, we found out that what was advertised as 30,000 km mileage was actually 130,000 because it was on its second time round! In spite of that the owner was asking 4,000 Euros for it.

While we were there we looked at a slightly younger Fiat Panda with a lower mileage. Robin made me get into the driving seat as he was determined I was going to drive on Crete. It was a comfortable driving position for me but I was unsure how

Robin would cope with his longer legs. The person showing us around said he could not sell us anything as he was just filling in for the garage owner. He took the Greek mobile number and said he would get the owner to call us. It was some time before we received a call and by that time we had decided we wanted to try and find something better for our money.

All was not lost as we went on to Chania and had a very nice day there. The weather was good. We had a walk round the town and a pleasant lunch looking over the harbour. I took photos to send home as it seemed unbelievable to be sitting outside in February!

After spending quite a lot of time trying to find some information online, I discovered that most of the used car dealers were in the Chania area. We decided to hire a car for the day again so that we could visit them. The man at the hire company found us a car that they were looking to sell and we hired it for the day to give it a test run. As usual, it was about ten years old and had a high mileage. Robin identified one or two potential problems, not least with the clutch as he had to physically lift his foot off the floor every time he had to depress it. We decided it was not something we wanted to spend our hard earned cash on.

We set off for Chania only to find that the car showrooms do not open on Saturdays. Rather than have another wasted journey, we decided we would have some lunch and then do some shopping. I wanted some dress fabrics and found them very expensive on Crete. I hoped they might be cheaper in Chania. We made the mistake of deciding to have lunch first, only to discover that, apart from those catering for tourists, the shops close at 2 p.m. Much to my regret, I have to admit

I gave poor Robin a hard time on the way home, complaining about what kind of country it was where the shops are closed on Saturday afternoons. I was so accustomed to shops being open seven days a week in the UK.

There is a car showroom just down the road from our apartment. We took a walk along there to see what was available. The asking price for the only car remotely suitable was 10,000 Euros which was more than we wanted to pay for a car of its age. We were beginning to despair that we would find anything suitable.

Shortly after this we went to Galero and the waiter told us about a second hand Fiat Panda his dealer had in the showroom that he thought we might be interested in. He told us to mention his name as he always bought his cars there. Once again, we hired a car for the day and went off to the dealer only to find it was the usual scenario. The car was ten years old and on its second time round the clock.

The salesman said he had a five year old Opel Corsa coming in in a few weeks' time priced at 8,000 Euros. Then he suggested we might want to consider buying new. For another 1,500 Euros we could buy a new Dacia Sandero. This seemed to make absolute sense. We would then have trouble free motoring for a few years and we would know exactly who had driven the car. The salesman said he had a white one coming in within the next few weeks. If we wanted another colour we would have to wait longer. We were not bothered about the colour so ordered the white one.

As usual, buying a new car on Crete involved a visit to the KEP office. It was in Robin's name so he had to take his passport and resident's permit, complete, sign and have witnessed a form. He was impressed when he went into the KEP office and the man behind the counter said, 'Good morning Mr Drawwater, how may I help you today?'

Not only did he remember Robin but he got our name right. Most people in the UK called us Drinkwater.

Next, we visited our accountant who told us we needed to pay for the car through our Greek bank account. If we paid direct from our UK account, there would be tax implications. It was a simple matter to transfer the money from our UK account to our Greek account. Then we had to go and queue in the Greek bank to have the money transferred to the car dealer's account.

When Robin went to the car dealer to sign all the documents to buy the car, he took a taxi and asked the taxi driver to wait. He was so disgusted at how much the taxi driver charged him, he decided go on foot to the showroom to take the document from the bank showing he had paid for the car. It was at least a six km walk there and back, if not more. He had been suffering from a cough he could not shake for a couple of weeks and had been to see a doctor. I remember him bounding into the apartment saying, 'There can't be much wrong with me if I can do that walk!'

The car was due to arrive at the end of March. We had arranged to visit the UK for Easter, which was at the beginning of April that year, so we agreed to collect the car on 5 April. I remember saying to Robin, 'I didn't think we would ever have another new car,'

and he replied, 'Ah, you never know what is going to happen.'

How prophetic that turned out to be.

The next job was to arrange insurance. We were recommended to an insurance broker in town who was very good.

He insisted on us sitting down for a chat and a coffee. Comprehensive insurance was quite expensive but we needed it with a new car. Also, it incorporated breakdown recovery which we paid extra for in the UK. We completed all the documents and arranged to call into the office to pay the premium the day before we were due to collect the car.

The March CIC lunch took place in a village just outside Rethymnon. A walk through the village and its surrounds was arranged beforehand and we both enjoyed it. Refreshment in the form of raki was provided along the way! Part of the walk involved a visit to a small local chapel where Robin and I both lit candles. Nick and Adrienne missed the walk, because they got lost en route, but were able to get to the lunch. I remember how excited Robin was at the prospect of getting the new car and he was telling Nick all about it.

Chapter 17 – Planning a visit to the UK

Now we had everything sorted out, it was time to plan a trip back to the UK. Direct flights from Chania to Gatwick were due to start at the end of March so we decided Easter would be a good time to visit.

This was one thing I was able to do easily online. It still took some time to find a suitable flight. I was trying to find a return flight where we would not have to be at the airport at some unearthly hour of the morning but I could not find one. The latest flight departed Gatwick at 8 a.m. The return fare was also significantly more expensive than for the flight out. Strangely, a flight with a changeover in Athens worked out cheaper overall than going direct, but we did not want to have to change flights, especially as we were only going for a few days. It also worked out cheaper to hire a car for the whole five days, and leave it in the airport car park, than to hire one just for one day at each end of the visit.

For the past few weeks Robin had had what we thought was a cold. It started with a blocked ear, which he managed to cure with the help of drops from the pharmacy and ear wash. Then he got a cough he could not shake. We thought nothing of it because when he got a cold it always went to his chest. He got some cough medicine from the pharmacist and something to bring up the phlegm from his chest. This helped but did not cure it. Much as we both hated going to see the doctor, he had no option.

The doctor was very thorough. He gave Robin a full ECG and told him his heart was healthy. His blood pressure was slightly raised but not enough to worry about. It is not unusual for the stress of seeing medical professionals to raise the blood pressure slightly, or it could have been the cough causing it. The doctor told him to monitor it and watch his salt intake.

Again, the antibiotics the doctor prescribed helped but did not cure the cough, so Robin had to go back. I remember that day well. Robin had an appointment in the evening. I was working, but I had a parcel to collect from the post office. We arranged that Robin would go to the doctor and I would go to the post office when I finished work. Then we would meet back home.

When I approached the post office, who should get up from the bench outside but Robin? He was in and out of the doctor's surgery quickly so decided to meet me instead of going home. He smiled at me and my heart did the little 'flip flop' it always did when I saw him, even after 43 years. The doctor could not understand why the antibiotics were not working so he wanted Robin to have a chest x-ray.

The next day was a busy one. On Crete, you do not make an appointment at the hospital for an x-ray. You go to a medical centre that carries out x-rays and blood tests. They usually do it straight away and give you the results to take to the doctor yourself. I had an appointment for a check-up with the dentist while Robin went for his x-ray. Then I had a hairdressing appointment. After that we met up at Galero.

I am not sure whether it was on this occasion or another. We had got to know one of the daytime waitresses at Galero quite well. She always remembered our names by thinking of

Robin Hood and Marilyn Monroe. On this occasion, she had been admiring a top I was wearing. I had knitted it myself from a cotton yarn and she was most impressed. Before she had even finished complimenting me on it, I managed to spill a cup of coffee all over me. It went everywhere, even down to my underwear. She sent me off to the ladies' to clean myself up, moved me to a dry seat and brought me a fresh coffee! It was still rather uncomfortable until I was able to go home and change. Thankfully, the coffee did not leave a permanent stain.

We had been to see the accountant in the morning. She needed a paper from the bank to show the money we had paid in to open the account, so we had to fit in another hour or so queuing in the bank. She said we could take the paper back in the afternoon so we went back about 2 p.m. and were told she would not be back until 5 p.m. We had forgotten here that a lot of businesses, not involved in the tourist industry, close around lunchtime and open again in the evening.

The medical centre was very busy so Robin had to go back in the evening to collect his x-rays. There was a very heavy dust storm that evening. It felt like something out of a science fiction movie. We could see the dust rolling in across the sea and the air turned orange. I made Robin tie a scarf round his face when we went back to the accountant and when he went to collect his x-rays to take them to the doctor. I did not want him breathing in the dust when he already had a cough. That was one of the few nights we did not walk into the town in the evening.

The x-rays proved to be clear much to relief of us both. In the UK Robin suffered from hay fever, so the doctor thought the cough might be the result of an allergy because Robin was not used to the climate. He gave Robin some more antibiotics, told him to enjoy his visit to the UK and to come back if the cough still did not clear up.

The following day the couple we met on New Year's Eve took us to the British Supermarket at Kalyves. We promised to return the compliment once we had picked up our car.

A couple of things stick in my mind from the following week, before we visited the UK. One was Robin saying that all through the summer he would be wearing just shorts, sandals and a T-shirt. The other was Robin putting his arms round me and saying, as he often did, 'We have something special, something not many couples have.'

I replied, 'I know and one day one of us will pay a heavy price for that,'

to which he replied, 'Not for years yet.'

At least I have the comfort of knowing he was looking forward to the summer and had no idea that he was dying. He also had a habit of saying, 'Have I told you I love you today? Well, I'll say it again so you don't forget.'

As if I could ever forget.

Karen had asked Robin to do the starter for our meals on Saturday and Sunday evenings, when the boys would be joining us. We still had our online shopping account with the UK supermarket, so we ordered the ingredients to be delivered to Karen, along with our contribution towards the Easter food and Easter eggs for the boys. Although the cost of living is lower on Crete, some items, such as deodorant, are quite expensive. There were also some cooking ingredients Robin wanted that we could not buy here. We got together and made a list of all the things we wanted to bring back with us.

We had been invited to meet our landlady and her partner for some wine and meze one evening before we left for the UK. Unfortunately, because I was working Monday to Wednesday and we were travelling on Thursday, there was too much for me to sort out and we could not make it. I wish we had now because it would have been one last enjoyable evening for Robin. I had to get the packing out of the way and all the other last minute chores such as washing. I remember putting a couple of machine loads of washing on the airing rack in the craft room. The weather was warm and sunny and I remember Robin saying, 'It'll all be dry by the time we get back.'

On Tuesday evening Robin asked me what I wanted for dinner the following day so he could make sure everything he needed was defrosted. We had bought some English sausages from the British supermarket and I remember saying, 'There are a couple of eggs that need using up before we go away, so let's have sausage, egg and chips.'

Out of all the exotic meals Robin had cooked over the years, the last meal he made for me turned out to be plain old sausage, egg and chips. He managed to make oven chips that tasted like proper ones. I have cooked a number of his recipes since he died but I have yet to master his oven chips. I cannot get them crispy like he did.

Chapter 18 – Our last visit to the UK

The next few chapters are hard for me to write but they are part of the story which needs to be told.

Although Robin and I really enjoyed travelling, especially to exotic places such as Vietnam and Malaysia, I have always found the preparation to be somewhat stressful. I have often had dreams where we were about to leave for the airport and I had not done the packing. Even though I always made a list and ticked things off as I packed them, I always worried I had forgotten something.

Then there was the nightmare that we might arrive at the airport without our passports, boarding passes, etc. I had seen it happen to people on television. On top of that, were the practical things like having my hair and nails done! Robin never had that problem. Working as a joiner meant a manicure was pointless. He liked to keep his hair short so he could just get out of the shower, towel it, comb it and it was almost dry. We both liked my hair long and even now, I still wear it shoulder length, but it does mean it takes a long time to dry.

On Maundy Thursday, everything checked and double checked to my satisfaction, we set off to collect our hire car. The man on the desk was a little puzzled that we had booked the car with an address on Crete but Robin's driving licence still had his UK address on it. However, he was satisfied when we explained that that was our address in the UK. We still owned the property and we were reluctant to give up our UK driving licences until we had to.

After returning to our apartment for our cases, we set off for the airport at Chania. For once, Robin's obsession with getting everywhere early stood us in good stead. We took a wrong turn on the way and had to double back on ourselves. We still arrived early and there was only one couple ahead of us at bag drop. Robin began chatting to them and was excited to tell them we now lived on Crete and were just returning to spend Easter with the family. The man replied, 'Doh, I didn't realise it was Easter, we're just going back for a visit.'

I could have hit him, but it did not dampen Robin's pleasure at being a Cretan resident.

Apart from the nagging cough, Robin seemed OK at the airport. He allowed himself a small beer with his sandwich in the cafe and was just thrilled to bits because we were only going back for a visit. For him, Crete was now home. I had my first inkling that things were not right when we were on the plane. When the stewardess came round to ask if we wanted drinks, Robin wanted a bottle of water. I asked if he wanted a Sprite zero, which is what he would normally have asked for, and he said, 'No, just water.'

The stewardess asked if he wanted a glass and he did not really seem to understand her and just shook his head. In the end, he hardly drank any of the water.

When we got to baggage reclaim he would normally be standing by the carousel waiting to grab the cases and pass them over to me. This time he had to sit down while we waited for the bags from our flight to come through. We had decided not to hire a car in the UK because it would just sit in Karen's parking space while we were there and seemed a waste of money. So we planned to take the train from Gatwick to Kingston. The station is just round the corner from Karen's flat. Neither of us really felt like getting on the train once we arrived at Gatwick, but the cost of a taxi was prohibitively expensive. That turned out to be a mistake.

As I have mentioned before, Robin did not travel well on public transport. We needed to change at Clapham Junction to get a train to Kingston but Robin did not last that long. He started sweating and I thought he was either going to pass out or vomit. This was not unusual but normally only on the underground when his claustrophobia kicked in. We had to get off at the next station and he sat on the platform, sweating profusely. After about ten minutes he said he felt better and was ready to resume our journey. However, by the time we got to Clapham Junction he said he could not face getting on another train and we got a taxi the rest of the way.

Once we got to Karen's flat he seemed back to normal. Zoe had cooked fajitas and we had a pleasant evening, drinking wine and talking. Unfortunately, the travelling combined with the wine caused me to wake up in the night with a migraine which kept me confined to bed most of Good Friday. I very much regret this now because Good Friday was the last day Robin was really well.

He took Karen shopping at the local supermarket and, as she later told me, he not only insisted on paying for her groceries, but on carrying them home as well. That was so typically Robin. At least I was able to get up and join Karen, Zoe and Robin for their evening meal, even though I was only able to eat toast. I felt really guilty because Zoe had been planning the meal for ages and made Teriyaki Salmon with her special salad.

By Saturday morning I was recovered and Robin seemed his normal self. I am so pleased that he was able to enjoy his full English breakfast, which was one of the things he had really been looking forward to. We went shopping to get the things on our list that we wanted to bring back with us. He needed plain T-shirts because he usually wore polo shirts in the UK but these would be too hot for a Cretan summer. The ones he usually took on holiday with him all carried the names of various places we had visited. He always brought a T-shirt back with him wherever we went.

I had also planned to make him some shorts. We bought him several T-shirts in various colours and then went to John Lewis to buy a shorts pattern and fabric. None of the shorts patterns were suitable because they were all too...short! He liked shorts that came down to his knees. By this time he was flagging and said to me, 'Marilyn, I'm knackered.'

He was not a great lover of shopping but this was unlike him.

We went back to Karen's flat for a snack lunch and, after a rest in the afternoon, he seemed a bit better. The boys were coming over for dinner and Robin was doing the starter. He managed that OK but was not able to eat very much dinner. As a youngster he could get through a large meal and finish off what everyone else left but, as he got older, his appetite diminished, so it did not really ring any alarm bells. Strangely enough, he managed to wade through a fair amount of Celebrations chocolates with his coffee! While relaxing after dinner he had a nose bleed that took a very long time to stop. Neither of us fancied spending hours at A & E and it did not appear to be anything serious.

During the night he was up several times which we again put down to a surfeit of chocolate. We had planned to go to mass at the local church on Easter Sunday but it was clear, after being up most of the night, that Robin was not well enough to attend mass. He seemed to rally a bit during the day but, by the evening, he was really struggling.

Normally, he would be as happy as anything pottering around in the kitchen, making the starter and interfering with the cooking. This time he really had difficulty preparing the starter and Karen and I ended up having to help him. He barely ate anything and could not even sit at the table for long. His excuse was that the dining chairs were uncomfortable on his skinny bottom. As usual, he thought of everyone else but himself and did not want to spoil everyone's Easter but letting on how ill he felt.

On Monday morning we went to do a bit of last minute shopping but, as we arrived at the supermarket, Robin said, 'I can't go any further, you go in and get what we need. I'll wait for you here.'

He had to sit on a bench outside. Karen came later to buy a few bits for Harvey and told me afterwards that she did not recognise Robin until he spoke to her and he was clearly jaundiced. She recognised that because Zoe had jaundice as a baby.

We had planned to spend the night at the Gatwick Travelodge because we had an early flight and did not want to disturb the rest of the family, when we had to get up before dawn to travel to the airport. By late afternoon, Robin was vomiting frequently and it soon became apparent that, despite his desperate wish to return to Crete, he was not well enough to travel. Trying to cancel the flight was a nightmare because, of course, it was a bank holiday. I was able to cancel the cab booked to take us to the airport hotel, just in time. Karen asked if I wanted her to contact the emergency doctor and I said yes.

Even though we explained the symptoms, the operator insisted on asking all the questions pertaining to a heart attack although it was clear he was not having a heart attack. It was fortunate Karen was speaking to the operator. I was very worried about Robin and my stress levels were through the roof, I would probably have been quite rude. Eventually they agreed to send the paramedics.

When they arrived and saw how weak and sallow Robin was, they immediately made arrangements for him to be taken to hospital. In his usual fashion when asked if he could walk to the ambulance, he said, 'Yes.' He could barely stand up and I had to get a bit harsh with him and tell him he couldn't possibly make it to the ambulance without assistance. I felt for him as he clearly saw it as an indignity having to be taken out in a wheelchair, but he really did not have any option.

Up to now he had told no-one he was vomiting and passing blood. We thought he just had diarrhoea and sickness. It was when he was sick in the ambulance and brought up blood that the paramedics blue-lighted him to A & E. In addition to whatever underlying problem was causing his cough, he now had sepsis although he did not know it at the time. Despite all this, he seemed to perk up once he was settled in a hospital bed. No doubt he was confident that whatever the problem was, he was in the best place to get it fixed. I can remember him saying, 'When I started coughing up blood, I thought I was a goner.'

Even at that stage, he clearly had no idea he was dying.

A blood test revealed a low platelet count and the doctor

was waiting for platelets from St George's Hospital to carry out a transfusion. As a result, Robin was not allowed anything to eat or drink and said he was hungry and thirsty. He was joking about wanting an egg sandwich and reaching out to towards a bottle of coke on the nurses' station and saying, 'Coke...coke.'

He told me to go back to Karen's flat, get a good night's sleep and he would see me in the morning.

By the time I arrived at the hospital the following morning, Robin had been for a CT scan. It had had a really bad effect on him and he said he passed out. He had deteriorated again overnight and had now been told he had sepsis. In addition, he had a deranged liver resulting from secondary cancer. The CT scan had been unable to assess the primary source. He was put into a medically induced coma because the sepsis was preventing any effective treatment for the cancer. Before he was put under sedation, a chart was completed, giving information such as name, date of birth, etc. Robin was also asked what was the most important thing in his life, simultaneously he said, 'My wife' and Karen said, 'Mum.'

He remained in a medically induced coma for the next four days. Apart from one quick visit when our son-in-law drove me to Karen's flat for a shower, I did not leave the hospital. The family brought in my wash kit and a change of clothes so I could freshen up. The staff kept telling me I needed to get some rest but I was afraid Robin would die while I was not there. The ICU staff were brilliant. They had a bed set up for me in the family room at night so that I could at least get a couple of hours rest. Proper sleep was out of the question.

They also kept nagging me to eat but I simply could not. Just the thought of trying to force food down my throat made me choke. Karen was bringing in smoothies and chocolate to keep me going.

I only had one complaint. Robin's full name was Christopher Robin. He found this embarrassing and had always been known as Robin from childhood, partly I suspect because he was born just before Christmas. Although his chart clearly showed his preferred name as Robin, some of the staff insisted on calling him Christopher, which I did find rather annoying. Had he been conscious and aware he would have hated it, as he would had he heard one of the nurses referring to him as elderly. Over seventy he might have been but elderly is a term that most certainly did not apply to Robin.

On the Wednesday morning the consultant said he could see how worried I was and that he could make a reasonable diagnosis based on the results of the CT scan before Robin had passed out. He said the ward rounds took place at 1.30 p.m. after which there would be a staff meeting. He would give me the prognosis then. He also suggested I might want a family member with me. That did not sound good.

Karen was not able to be with me because Harvey was on holiday from school so our younger daughter, Nicky, and Craig, her husband, arranged to be there. Following the ward round and staff meeting, the consultant told me he had one other person to see and then would come to the family room to speak with us. It turned out that he actually saw several other people. After intimating he had bad news for us, he then left us waiting for two and a half hours. Nicky said afterwards that the clock had a 'tick' missing and she would always remember how irritating it was.

When he finally came to see us, the consultant told me that

Robin had cancer of the small cells and there was very little chance of survival. He also said there was a clot on his lung and, if he stopped breathing, they would not resuscitate him. I had never heard of small cell cancer before and do not think I quite took it in. The saying goes 'where there's life, there's hope' and all the time Robin was still breathing, I thought he might prove them all wrong. He was strong and had fought illness before, he would do the same now. I even went to the hospital chapel for a short time each day to pray for his survival.

On Friday morning a new consultant came on duty for the weekend. He was much more pleasant than the first. He gave us a small ray of hope by saying that the cancer was not curable but it was treatable. The sepsis was now under control, so Robin was moved out of isolation and into the main ICU. I was told I could not stay with him all the time because it would disturb other patients. Because I had been given a glimmer of hope, I was able to go back to Karen's flat, have a decent meal, a shower and a good night's sleep.

Robin was being brought round from his coma and when I called on the Friday evening the phone was put to his ear. The nurse told me Robin opened his eyes when he heard my voice. Buoyed up by hope I was able to straighten my hair and put on make-up before going to the hospital the following morning. I am so glad I did this because that was the last view of me that Robin had. At least I had the chance to say 'I love you' one last time.

We all believed that Robin was being brought out of his coma so that he could start treatment but I am sure, looking back, that it was so he could say goodbye to his family. It was clear from when I first arrived at the hospital that he was struggling to breathe. It was heartbreaking to see this once big, strong, man begging me to help him, and there was nothing I could do except hold his hand.

It was typical of Robin that he made people laugh right to the last. He had had nothing by mouth in almost a week. The nurse said he could have a cup of tea which he was able to drink through a straw. Before he was given it, the nurse said, 'Robin, if you want a cup of tea, you have to open your eyes.'

He was so keen to get his cup of tea that his eyes shot wide open. This was related to, and amused, all the nursing staff!

By late afternoon, not only was he struggling to breathe but his heart rate and blood pressure had risen to dangerous levels. One of the junior doctors was called and she said he would have to be put back under sedation. The last thing I remember him saying to me was, 'What brought this on?'

I had no answer, all I could say was, 'I don't know, my love.'

I had to wait in the family room while he was sedated and was told I could go back when that had been done. I do not know how long I waited but it seemed like hours. Eventually, a nurse came out and told me he was very sick and, if any family members wanted to see him, they would have to get there quickly. Fortunately, I had Karen's number programmed into my phone because I was shaking so much I could never have dialled it. In the end, the nurse had to speak to Karen because I could not get the words out.

I was desperate to get back to Robin but I was still not allowed in. I was pacing up and down the family room begging a god I no longer believe in not to take Robin away from me. Finally, I was allowed back. The doctor was using some kind of hand pump to breathe air into Robin's lungs. I think he was telling me he wanted permission to stop trying but I could not make that decision, so he put Robin back on the ventilator. Most of the family were able to get there by the time the doctor said the worst thing I have ever heard in my life, 'That's it, his heart has stopped.'

The most important thing to me was that I was with him and holding his hand when he died.

Chapter 19 – The Aftermath

It is said that the road to hell is paved with good intentions. That is certainly true when someone suffers the loss of a loved one. People come out with the most unbelievable rubbish in the hope it will make you feel better when, in fact, it makes you feel worse. I was amazed at how many people, some of whom had never even *met* Robin, could tell me what he would want. They say they are sorry for your loss, and mean it, but it does not help. Worst of all was being told 'life goes on' or 'that's life' as if losing the love of that life was an everyday occurrence, like going to the supermarket or vacuuming the carpet, and mattered just as little. Most couples, especially in the twentieth century, continue their lives as individuals. Robin and I were so close we became almost like one person. Without him, part of me will always be missing.

Somehow Karen, Zoe, Craig, Nicky and I managed to pile into Craig's car to get from the hospital to Karen's flat. Fortunately, Harvey was at overnight respite so we had a chance to get over our initial trauma before trying to explain to him that his Granddad had died. We were all in shock. From Good Friday, when he appeared to be his normal self, laughing, joking and enjoying a glass of wine, in just over a week he was gone. He was not even an old man. All his family lived to a grand old age. I could not help but feel he had been cheated.

For the next few days I was like a sleepwalker. I just could not take it in. It was an effort just to get out of bed. I had always taken care with my appearance but just having a shower and getting dressed was a monumental effort. I could not care less what I wore and did not bother with any make-up. The fact that I would never be seen outside the house without make-up had previously caused some of our rare arguments.

On the following Monday we had to go and register the death. I just did not feel I could do it. Karen had to get quite stern with me to get me to the Register Office. Once the formalities were out of the way, I was able to visit Robin in the mortuary. The mortuary staff had dressed him in a purple gown and it reminded me of when he used to be sub-deacon in church. He looked just like he was asleep. He was not even as cold as I expected him to be. I sat with him for a while, just stroking his hair. Even at seventy-two he still had a full head of hair with very little grey. He was proud of that.

Zoe offered to meet Harvey from school so that Karen and I could go and have some lunch and a couple of glasses of wine. We went to the Albert pub which is near the hospital. I remember years ago when my father was undergoing surgery at Kingston Hospital. We would take my mother to visit him in the evening and then go on to the Albert (or Prince Albert as it was called then). Dad knew where we were going and would say, 'You rotten lot, I could murder a pint!'

Of course by this time I had become used to Crete prices and was stunned at the cost of a large glass of wine.

Craig offered to organise the funeral for me and I will always be grateful to him for that. There was no way I was in any fit state to do it myself, although I knew what Robin wanted. A couple of days later we visited the undertaker. Craig had taken the trouble to find someone we knew. We had gone to the same church and her son was in the Cubs and Scouts when we ran them. It was agreed that a priest from Plumstead would conduct the service but it would take place at St. Luke's Church in Kingston. That was more accessible to people who would want to attend.

The priest from Plumstead and the parish priest from St Luke's were both personal friends and fellow members of the Order of St John. Unfortunately, it took quite some arranging to find a date when both priests and the undertaker were all available. The date could not be fixed until the end of April. Craig, Karen and Nicky took me for a drink afterwards - a large gin and tonic. I recall Craig saying, 'The answer's gin and tonic, what's the question?'

It did make me feel better, at least temporarily.

Even choosing the hymns and readings was difficult. Making any kind of decision seemed almost impossible. I do remember choosing Lord of all Hopefulness especially. This always reminded me of Robin because there is a line in one of the verses that says, 'His strong hands were skilled with the plane and the lathe.'

In the meantime, there were so many things to sort out. Nicky lent me her laptop so that I could continue doing some work and, strangely enough, I was able to concentrate on that.

I had to get the house sorted out because I needed to get it rented. It was held in such a way that Robin's share automatically passed to me on his death. All I had to do was download a form from the internet and send it to the Land Registry with a copy of the death certificate. Similarly, with our joint bank accounts, all I needed to do was take a copy of the death certificate into the branch and they were transferred into my sole name in minutes. It was heartbreaking how he could be wiped out so easily. It was almost as if he had never existed.

I am certainly thankful for the 'tell us once' service where I completed a form online and all relevant authorities were automatically notified, such as the Pensions Agency, the Passport Office and the DVLA. I was also allowed to keep Robin's passport and his driving licence so long as I rendered them unusable.

It was Karen who gave me the idea of putting them in a memory box for Robin. She had done the same when her daughter, Natasha, died at just fourteen months of age, only a few years previously. Robin and Craig had carried her coffin and Robin said afterwards that it was one of the most difficult things he had ever had to do. It did seem that our family was being hit by one tragedy after another.

I now entered into a state of limbo. There was nothing much more I could do until after the funeral. Even if I decided not to stay on Crete, I knew I would have to go back because, apart from our house in Surbiton, everything I owned was there. The thought of making that journey alone was something I was not yet able to contemplate.

The undertaker had made enquiries with the Greek Embassy to find out what I needed to do to take Robin's ashes back to Crete. I was told I needed formalised copies of the death and cremation certificates. I would then need to take the urn containing Robin's ashes, together with these documents and Greek translations, to the Greek embassy to have an official seal put on them. I posted a copy of the death certificate to our Greek accountant because she had had a copy of our marriage certificate translated for us. She was able to return it fairly quickly and I posted it off to the Foreign Office and received the formalised copy before the funeral.

Karen was also put under a lot of pressure regarding the funeral. She arranged for Harvey to have an extra overnight respite stay on that day. Everything was arranged for him to be collected from school on the day before the funeral and taken to his overnight respite. He would then be taken to school the following morning and return home in the evening as normal.

Karen wrote everything out and handed it over to the local authority, his escort and the transport service that took him to school. I lost count of the number of telephone calls she received asking her to confirm the arrangements. Even on the morning of the funeral she received a call asking where Harvey needed to be collected from. She had provided this information numerous times and I do not know how she kept her temper.

For some reason Robin's body was only able to be transferred to the funeral director a couple of days before the funeral. I was asked if I wanted to go and see him one last time. As he had looked so peaceful in the mortuary, I said yes. I was not prepared for what I would see. I had provided a full suit of clothes including underwear, shoes, socks and the set of cufflinks his sister bought him for Christmas that he never got to wear. I had arranged for him to be embalmed so it was a complete shock to see his face so grey and sunken. He looked like something out of a horror film. Either the embalming had not worked or it had been done too late. That was not my Robin, I could not stay. I wanted to remember him as he was in life.

I had arranged for Robin's body to be in the church overnight and Craig took me along for a short service to greet his arrival.

It all still seemed so unreal.

On the morning of the funeral, I was somehow able to get myself together. I had left one of my business suits with Karen so I was able to wear that. Somehow I managed to do my hair and put on make-up. I owed that to Robin. It was heart-warming to see so many people in church. As well as family, there was a large contingent from the Order of St John in full regalia, several people from the church we attended before moving to Crete and people who knew us from St. Luke's, even Robin's accountant made the effort. There were more people at the funeral than normally attended Sunday mass.

It was a full requiem mass and four priests were at the altar, in addition to the two already mentioned, there was the parish priest from our old church and another who had served at the altar with Robin before being ordained. Now was the time that it started to hit me that he was really dead. I kept looking at the coffin and thinking the man I love is in there. I had a lot of support from family and friends. After the church service, I followed the hearse to the parish boundary along with the Knights and Dames of St. John. Close family only went on to the crematorium where we had another short service.

I remembered another friend who had died young. She had a beautiful voice. Robin had always said he wanted her to sing *Panis Angelicus* at his funeral. Because she was no longer able to do this, we played a recording of it by Katherine Jenkins, of whom Robin was a great fan.

I had reserved a private room at the Druid's Head in Kingston for the funeral party. Again, this was Karen's suggestion. It is the oldest pub in Kingston and Robin and I had often walked along the river from Surbiton to have Sunday lunch there. She thought it was where Robin would want it to be held. Not everyone was able to attend but there were a good few people there. The numbness came back to me again that evening. That was probably because everyone wanted to talk to me and I must admit I downed quite a few glasses of wine.

Over the next few weeks Karen was very good to me. She did all my washing and tried to find tasty treats to re-awaken my non-existent appetite. We spoke about Robin all the time and grew close over those weeks in the same way that I had with my own mother after my father died.

But the strain was beginning to tell. Harvey could not quite grasp the idea that Robin was dead but he clearly knew something was wrong. He was having meltdowns at home and hitting other children at school, which was most unlike him. Karen and I ended up having an enormous row. It was clearly a result of the stress we were both under and I cannot even remember what it was about, but it made me realise that I had to make a decision about what I was going to do. Robin and I had travelled at the end of March intending to stay five days and I had been with Karen for almost two months.

I sent off the cremation certificate to the Foreign Office for formalisation only to receive it back with a letter to say it was not an official document like the death certificate, so I would need to get it notarised. This was the final straw. I realised that I did not need a pot of ashes to remember Robin by. He would always be with me in spirit wherever his ashes were. I asked Karen if she would mind keeping them and she said of course not.

Karen had suggested asking the undertaker for a lock of Robin's hair and I am really glad I did. She cut quite a large piece so I was able to give some to Karen, put some in a locket which I always wear and keep some in a silver box I bought. I also decided I could put a few of his ashes in the box in my suitcase. Wherever Robin was, I could imagine him laughing at me scooping a few of his ashes out of the urn with a teaspoon! People have since asked me why I did not just put his ashes in my suitcase. I could not do that. Imagine how I would have felt if they had been confiscated.

EasyJet had given me a credit for the flight I had to cancel so I was able to re-arrange a flight back to Crete without any extra cost. The couple we had met on New Year's Eve kindly offered to pick me up at the airport when I arrived back in Crete. I arranged for a taxi to take me to the airport, packed my single suitcase and told Karen to give Robin's suitcase and its contents to a charity shop. Before my return to Crete, I took Karen out to lunch as a thank you. We went to Los Iguanas, another of Robin's favourite places, and had all the tapas dishes he enjoyed. We even sat at the same table we had shared the last time we had been there with Robin.

The taxi was due to collect me early on the morning of my flight and I was terrified. I had travelled on my own before but not under these circumstances. At the height of my panic, I felt a strange sense of calm and am sure Robin was giving me the strength I needed. Usually, once we had dropped off our hold luggage, we would have breakfast but I could not face the thought of food. I kept remembering travelling with Robin when he would say, 'I'll take care of the cases, and you sort out the paperwork.'

He would drag both suitcases through bag drop and onto the conveyer while I dealt with the passports and boarding passes.

That was a nightmare journey. There was a safety issue that had to be resolved before we could take off. Then we missed our slot and had to wait for another. In all, we were sat on the tarmac for about two hours. The seatbelt signs went on and off several times. To add to the misery, I was sat next to a couple with a small child who screamed every time her seatbelt was put on. Eventually we got on our way and I texted the couple who were collecting me to let them know I would be at least two hours late.

Once we had taken off, the flight was uneventful. I fortified myself with a large gin and tonic and was able to manage a snack box. Landing at Heraklion was heart rending. This was the first time I had exited the plane into the bright Cretan sunshine without feeling a sense of excitement. Until our move to Crete, we had always flown to Heraklion so it was very familiar. I could easily picture Robin waiting by the carousel to retrieve our cases. I would stand behind him but out of the way. He would then pass me the first one to wheel away while he waited for the other. This time there was just me and one case.

My friends were waiting for me after I went through the nothing to declare section and gave me a big hug. They kindly stopped at a nice place for coffee on the way home from the airport. It was lovely, right on the beach beside the incredibly blue Cretan sea, but I just wanted to get it over with. I had no idea how I would feel once I got back to the apartment without Robin.

When we arrived at the apartment, my friends offered to come in with me. I was really afraid of going in on my own. At first it did not seem too bad. Everything was not overwhelming me, which was what I had expected. My friends asked if

I needed anything and I said I did not because I intended to eat out that evening. It was now late afternoon so I unpacked, showered and changed. Then I walked across to the Sunset Taverna for some food. I still felt reasonably buoyant. I think it was because I was in the place Robin loved so much and was probably helped by a couple of glasses of wine, but I was thinking, I can do this, I can carry on Robin's dream for him.

Chapter 20 – Carrying on Robin's dream

It was the next day when it really hit me that I was now alone on Crete without Robin.

Sadness flooded me. Robin had to wear rubber gloves to wash up because washing up liquid caused the psoriasis on his hands to flare up. His dishwashing gloves were hanging up next to mine. Usually I would wash and he would dry. The tea towel he had used to dry the dishes following our last meal was still hanging up to dry. On the coffee table were the sketches he had made of the things he wanted to make in his workshop, along with the English translation of the specifications for our new car. I could remember him poring over them and saying, 'This may only be a cheap little car but it has everything on it.'

The airing rack in the spare bedroom had all his dry boxer shorts, socks and polo shirts on it. His toiletries were in the bathroom and on the dressing table. Instead of perfume I started wearing the Dolce & Gabbana cologne his sister had bought him. The bottle was open so I could not give it to a charity shop but I did not want to throw it away. Even the table was still set for two. Everything was as he had left it waiting for him to come back, even though he would never come back again.

I kept asking myself how our dream had turned into such a nightmare. We had spent years planning the move to Crete, but instead of enjoying life and growing old together, I was now all alone. I have to admit I was more than a little afraid.

Even going to the supermarket was difficult. I needed some shampoo and conditioner. Looking at the toiletries section, I could not help noticing all the things Robin used to buy, such as shaving foam and razors. All the labels were in Greek and I could not work out which was shampoo and which was conditioner. I came close to bursting into tears and collapsing in a heap on the floor.

The first thing I had to do was to go to see our landlady and let her know I was back. We cried together and she assured me Robin is always with me in spirit. I also needed to visit the hairdresser whose salon is opposite the shop. By this time I was beginning to realise that I should start taking care of my appearance both for myself and to honour Robin's memory. My landlady was a great support to me in those early months. I called into her shop almost every day and would sit, cry and talk to her about Robin. She did not try to tell me to let go and move on, just listened to me and told me he is always with me.

The next thing I had to do was sort out the car. Before going to the UK we had put aside the money for the car insurance so we could pay the broker prior to collecting the car. Before I could do that, I had to get ownership transferred into my name because the car had been purchased in Robin's name. This was quite a simple procedure but it will come as no surprise that it entailed another visit to the KEP Office to have the transfer form witnessed. The friends who collected me from the airport took me to the car showroom, then the KEP Office and back again. The car salesman would have arranged for someone to drive me there, had my friends had not been with me.

I was told it would be about a week before ownership was transferred into my name. In the meantime, I paid the insurance. The broker was very kind. He said he had only met Robin a couple of times but thought he was 'a great guy.' On several occasions we had seen a cycle with a completely wooden frame about town. With his interest in anything made out of wood, Robin had been fascinated with it. Strangely enough, it turned out to belong to our insurance broker.

Sadly, I have lost touch with the friends who collected me from the airport. They were very supportive and took me out for a couple of meals but I think there were aspects of my grief they found hard to cope with. Because they were quite elderly, I could understand that. At this time, Adrienne was meeting me for coffee at least once a week, just to check that I was OK. On the day I collected the car she came into town on the bus and sat in the passenger seat when I drove back from the garage, to give me some confidence. I certainly needed the moral support.

Due to a combination of grief, not having driven for some time and never having driven on the right, my first efforts were not brilliant. For some reason, I kept driving too close to the right and hitting the kerb. It says a lot for Adrienne that she braved taking me out for a number of driving lessons before I started to build up some confidence! In life Robin was a terrible back seat driver, but I was glad of that when I felt he was watching over me and helping me. When we first moved to Crete, I can remember him saying to me, 'It's quite easy to drive on the right, but you'll probably try to change gear with the door handle the first few times.'

How right he was, it seemed so strange to be changing gear with my right hand, even though I am right handed!

What to do with Robin's tools was a dilemma. They meant

a great deal to him and were very much part of his personality. I could not just throw them away but selling them would be difficult because they would all need adaptors to change from the UK three pin system to the Greek two pin system. In the end I hit on the idea of sending them to his son in the UK. I asked if he would like them and he said he would treasure them, so I arranged for the company that shipped our goods over here to collect them and deliver them to Robin's son. I am sure Robin approved of my decision.

Adrienne also helped me to donate some of Robin's clothes to her friend who runs a dog rescue centre. She could sell them at car boot sales to raise much needed funds. One or two people were quite shocked that I was able to do this so soon. I had little choice. We shared the wardrobes. Winter clothes were in our bedroom, holiday clothes were in the wardrobe in the craft room and summer clothes were in the guest bedroom. Every time I went to the wardrobe to get my clothes out, there were Robin's haunting me.

I did keep one or two things. They went into his memory box with things like the order of service from his funeral and his swimming and lifesaving certificates. I put the shoes he was so pleased to have repaired in there, along with the tracksuit top that had his swimming, canoeing and lifesaving badges sewn onto it. I still have his blazer with the badge of the Order of St John on it. In addition, I have altered to fit me the last two nice holiday shirts he bought and I wear them often.

When I first returned to Crete, I found that I wanted to spend as little time in the apartment as possible. I was eating out every day, both at lunchtime and in the evening because I found cooking for myself difficult. It was all too easy to visualise

Robin pottering about in the kitchen. This did nothing for my bank balance or my waistline.

Before our visit to the UK, places that close during the winter were getting ready to open up for the season. Robin was so looking forward to visiting the tavernas where we were known and telling the staff we were now resident in Rethymnon. I remember him saying it would be difficult to stick to our no alcohol during the week routine when people were pressing free drinks on us. By the time I came back, the season was in full swing.

There was no shortage of places where I could get a meal for a reasonable price. Going back to places where I went with Robin was very hard. The first time I went to Chaplin's for a snack, the waitress asked me if Robin was shopping and I had to explain that he had died. She was shocked but told me to be strong. I felt anything but strong.

The place we probably went most frequently was Galero, both for lunchtime snacks and a drink in the evenings, soft drinks during the week and wine at weekends. Our landlady said when she told the girl who worked behind the bar that Robin had died, she cried and was most anxious to see me. It took me a while to pluck up courage to go to Galero. The bar tender put her arms round me and stroked my hair while I cried. She said that when someone you do not know very well dies, you do not usually remember what they look like. With Robin, she could clearly picture him sitting on the bar stool.

The daytime waitress was also upset when I went for a snack at lunchtime and had to tell her, as was the owner of the cafe. There is also the Rimondi Restaurant opposite which is attached to Galero but closes in the winter. Robin had said we would have to go there for a meal once it opened, so I went there a number of times during that first summer.

I knew I had to go back to the seafood restaurant and tell our friend there what had happened. This was difficult because we had gone there for our celebration meal after putting everything in place to move to Crete. As with so many other people, he was shocked. He remembered the big, strong man who offered to help with his redecoration. He bought me a drink and then came over with the bottle and said, 'We will drink to the spirit of my friend.'

Everyone knows everyone in Rethymnon and word soon got round. Wherever I went people came to speak to me and say how sorry they were.

The final thing I had to sort out was my tax declaration. I had sent a copy of Robin's death certificate to our accountant from the UK so this had been translated and lodged at the town hall. I found the meeting with the accountant very difficult because she kept saying; 'Now your husband is no longer alive.'

Although it was clearly the truth, it was certainly not something I needed to be reminded of.

Adrienne made some enquiries through the CIC and found some ladies' groups I could join so I would not feel so isolated. I started going to a group that meets in a cafe on Thursday mornings called The Makers. They had originally met to make blankets and other things for the Red Cross but, when these were no longer needed, they continued to meet and bring along their own projects. I also went to a few lunches with a group started by another lady who had been widowed suddenly. She told me the grief eases with time but, even after fifteen years, it still sometimes hit her with the force of a freight train. I found that a breath of fresh air after people telling me I should let go and move on.

The word 'soulmate' tends to be bandied around every time someone has a new infatuation, but Robin and I were true soulmates. Another friend said that you only have one soul, so you can only have one soulmate. I found that comforting when so many people seemed to think I could just forget Robin and find someone else. Sadly, I have also mostly lost contact with that friend. Sometimes I think, when friends come and go, that they are sent to us for a while when we most need them but, as far as I am concerned, my door is always open to all the friends I have lost contact with.

Adrienne and Nick took me out for a meal every now and again and I still meet with them frequently. I was, and still am, very grateful for their friendship. After all, they had not known us for very long. Before coming back to Crete, I had had some discussions with the family regarding the possibility of moving back to the UK. Once I had returned to Crete, the prospect of returning to the UK even for a visit seemed beyond me. The thought of packing everything up and moving back made me feel physically sick. Over time I came to realise that I wanted to stay and carry on our dream. Work was a lifeline at this time. I changed my hours from three days a week to four hours a day in the afternoons.

The real turning point came when I got my little dog, Pokio. I wanted to adopt a stray dog but decided to wait until the weather cooled down a bit and the town was less crowded. By the end of September, I came to the decision that the time was right. Adrienne took me to meet her friend who ran the rescue centre. She had several dogs at home but they were all too big for me to keep in an apartment. Then she told me about a small dog she had heard of that had been dumped in a field.

She took me to the farmer's field and I fell in love with the little dog straight away. The only thing that worried me was that he had quite large feet. I thought he was a puppy and would grow to be a large dog. Adrienne looked at his teeth and estimated he was about 18 months old, so fully grown. He has Beagle ears and Basset feet, what else is in the mix I cannot hazard a guess! He has the most gorgeous big brown eyes, just like Robin.

I had hoped that someone in need could make use of the remainder of Robin's clothes. To this end Adrienne kindly agreed to contact the Greek Red Cross for me. It was disappointing when they said they had no room to store them and advised me to put them in the recycling bins. As I have said before, Robin was a smart man and liked his clothes. The thought of putting them in the recycling bin was very upsetting. As a result, we took the rest to the rescue centre when I went to collect my dog.

The lady had very kindly arranged for all his vaccinations. She would have arranged to have him neutered, which is a requirement on Crete when adopting an animal. This would have meant that I could not officially adopt him until the surgery had been carried out. I said I could afford to pay to have it done so I would arrange for it myself.

I wanted to choose a name that would have a connection with Robin but calling a dog Rob or Robin would be just plain silly. Pokio was a nickname Robin had acquired. One day I was using my laptop on the dining table in our house in the UK, when Robin kept asking, 'What are you doing?'

In the end, I said, 'You are so nosy!'

He replied, 'Yes, I have a big long nose like Pokio,' meaning of course Pinocchio.

That really made me laugh and the name stuck, I was his Sunshine and he was my Pokio.

Gradually over the weeks as Pokio settled in and we got to know each other, I found I was able to spend more time at home and actually cook for myself. Now I only eat out at weekends and on special occasions. Most places here are dog friendly so when I go out for a meal or a drink; I am able to take Pokio with me. Wherever I go people say hello to Pokio first and me afterwards! If I leave him at home, the first question is always, 'Where's Pokio?'

He is quite a local celebrity and has certainly helped me deal with my loneliness. One or two of my friends think he was sent to me by Robin to help me cope with my loss. Pokio and I have also joined a walking group. We meet at a village just outside Rethymnon, go on a long but fairly easy walk and then adjourn to the local taverna for lunch. Robin would have enjoyed it very much, he loved the local food and the atmosphere.

I still keep in regular touch with Adrienne and Nick and have gradually built up a circle of friends who meet on a regular basis. Another part of our plan was to learn to speak at least some basic Greek. This is proving far more difficult than expected but I am persevering. It is not the life I envisaged spending with Robin but I manage to keep busy.

Several people have told me I should not rule out finding someone else. Indeed, I have been told that Robin would not want me to cut off that part of my life. I am sure that is right and he would understand, but what we shared was so special I could never re-create it with anyone else. One thing I have learned since Robin's death is that you do not stop loving someone just because they die. My love for him is just as strong now as it was when he was alive.

Robin gave me the most wonderful forty-three years any woman could ask for and I will always be grateful for that. We had love, laughter and happiness. It would be nice to have a companion I could share a meal or go to the cinema with. But that person could only ever be second best and that would not be fair on any man. I simply could not imagine sharing my home, and certainly not my bed, with someone else.

Sometimes I do get lonely and crave Robin's physical presence. There are days when I long just to feel his arms around me and hear him say some of the silly things that made me laugh.

Living alone is not easy for someone who has been happily married for most of her adult life. Even when undertaking tasks I would normally have done myself I miss being able to discuss them with Robin. Dealing with Greek bureaucracy was hard enough when there were two of us. There have been numerous occasions when I have been under stress, afraid and worried about what to do when he has managed to give me the answer. Just thinking about him and what he would advise gives me the strength to deal with the difficulties.

Since losing Robin, I have become more spiritually enlightened. Even when I went to church on a regular basis, I do not think I was as aware of something outside this life as I am now. Robin is always with me in spirit and in my heart.

There were things Robin used to say that sometimes drove me mad at the time, such as, 'Don't worry about tomorrow until it gets here,' or, 'Live for today, you don't know what's round the corner.'

I realise now how wise he was and I try not to worry about things that are not likely to happen or are months in the future.

Of course, a psychologist would tell me that this is just unresolved grief and that when I "get over" Robin's death there will be no more sense that he is sending me spiritual messages. They are entitled to their opinion and are no doubt very learned but I know what I feel. Friends and family have also felt Robin's presence from time to time. It is difficult to understand why people are so reluctant to believe there is something outside this life. It seems to me that believing in an afterlife is the only thing that makes sense of this one!

I have the most wonderful memories to sustain me and I feel Robin's love surrounding me. As he used to say himself, what more do I need?

I will always miss Robin but Crete will not be our last big adventure together. I just have to wait until my earthly journey ends for the next one to begin.

THE END

Acknowledgements

Most of the factual information in this book regarding the various festivals on Crete has been obtained online from www.explorecrete.com (accessed 2020). I would like to thank The Writers Bureau and, in particular, my tutor Sheila Bugler. Had I not undertaken their Creative Writing Course, I would never have had the idea of putting Robin's and my experiences into book form.

Thanks also to Charlotte Mouncey of www.bookstyle.co.uk for the cover design and to The Conrad Press Ltd. for publishing this book.